Buttons' Journey

My First 2 Years Living with PTSD

LaResse Harvey

DEDICATION

This book is dedicated to my children, Asiana and O'Bee; my
grandchildren, Dayne, Marleigh, and Keegan. We create our own legacies.
To my Auntie Karen and Uncle Bosco, you are always with me.
Love you all and thank you for loving me.

CONTENTS

ACKNOWLEDGMENTS

I would like to thank the following people for helping me to make this book possible. Taurus, first cousins are like siblings. Thank you for being a big brother to me. You gave me the laptop that started it all. Annette, I could not ask for a better woman for Taurus. Your continued encouragement and advice strengthen me on some of my worst days.

To my beautiful loving sisters, Semadar and Amazetta. You welcome me with open arms and showered me with love. Amazetta, thank you for being my life-line. My niece, Myeisha, you loved me and pushed me to be better. Thank you for that.

Maurice, my brother and spiritual friend. I cannot thank you enough for all the prayers, conversations, and healing advice.

To my dear friends the Butlers, James and Janice. You were there to pick me up. Your love and support helped me to get to a safe place to heal. I will never forget your kindness.

A special thank you to my editors Dr. V. Sims (1st draft) and T. Cooper (final draft).

Introduction

Greetings friends, old and new. Today I would like to share something with you. I want to invite you to take a glimpse into my life story. I will pull back the blinds, so you can see what's in the past, buried away and longing to be revealed. My hope, by sharing my life experiences, is that you may identify with some things, or least understand them. I want to share this journey with YOU. Perhaps somewhere along this journey, you and I can come to a place of knowing. I want to be able to freely reveal not only my strengths but my weaknesses too. Throughout, you will come to know the many characters from my life. And yes, every one of them is real. Of course, for legal purposes, I have changed the names, even though they left a real imprint on my life, my truth. The only real names used will be ones of a few family members. Also let me warn you, often in writing my story I express myself in modern "text talk", like LOL (laughing out loud) and SMH (shaking my head). Just me "keeping it real" and honest.

I will try not to bore you. But most importantly I hope that this journey teaches you to be gentle yet honest with yourself. Writing this book has taught me the importance of those lessons. I see now in hindsight how my emotions and actions took center stage in my life. I'm aware that when my actions and emotions don't match up, there is a problem. Through much introspective work, I have learned to recognize that when this happens one of two things is happening. One, I'm a creature of positive change. My emotions are changing; however, my reactions and response haven't quite caught up yet. Or, the second reason, is that I'm faking my emotions and actions to manipulate a situation. This one is tricky because it can happen intentionally or out of unintentional "survival mode" habit. Much of my life I've learned to operate in this "survival mode" function, with very little true success. One's true self is always brewing just beneath the surface. The more you try to push it back down, the greater the war within becomes.

Today I am consciously working to win that war. Daily I affirm that I am not a victim but a victor. I have the right to love myself. I have the right to have honest feelings. I have the right to expose bruises and all. I am here because I am purposed to be here. And so are you.

This is a journey. This book is my life's journey, of then, now and God willing, what will be. I am allowing you to see a glimpse of my fully-exposed Divine self. This is the part of me that is love and light. As we know, where truth exists love and light prosper. I know this sounds a little spiritual, because it is. I embrace the Spiritual Laws that teach me "why?" and lessons to learn before one dies. Now I must confess, I am still learning as I retell this story. I truly don't know the extent of my learning, where the road will lead me. But I am willing to give my truth in exchange for that love and light.

I try to acknowledge the many challenges I must overcome. Every morning I look in the mirror and declare, "I Love You." This is a must. I am in my forties, a mother of two, grandmother of three, and the second oldest of four children. I am an advocate, community organizer and grassroots lobbyist. Nothing about me is by happenstance. I have endured severe emotional and physical traumas that have resulted in chronic PTSD, depression, anxiety and a seizure disorder. When I decided that I would commit to this journey, I was 18-months into my new life as a person with mental illness. But I am here.

I overcame my darkest moments which gives me hope. I constantly remind myself I am a beautiful powerful woman. I hope I can help you or a loved one by telling my story. The truth is, knowing that I am not alone is soothing to my soul. It is comforting to know that people are willing to learn about non-veteran Post Traumatic Stress Disorder. When loved ones understand and recognize triggers and emotional outbursts, it's liberating. No longer do I have to suppress or hide my emotions. I am learning to grow through the trauma. I am learning that my intellect, education and professional savvy couldn't keep me from feeling the pain from my past. Feeling lost, alone and alienated. My mind longed for peace, but peace seemed a distant fantasy, unreachable for me. But through much therapeutic work, support and meditative practices, hope was revealed.

Hope is the key to overcoming any adversity. As I climb to the top of my new life through this book, I hold onto hope. For you, I hope you too will discover how to find peace in the midst of chaos. Peace is being happy with oneself and being true. I hope in sharing my story, you too will reckon with your true you. Don't worry, I'll be right here to help you along the way. Now please enjoy Button's Journey.

Just A Thought

By LaResse Harvey 5/19/06

Sometimes all we need is just a thought.........

Someone who thinks of us and calls just to say hello.

Someone who will send a friendly email with a smile, to let you know... You were on their mind.

Sometimes all we want is just a thought..............

Someone to hold us and whisper poetry into our ears.

Someone to lay next to without fears of performing.

Someone to talk to who really understands.....

Just a thought...........

Of someone who cares will take you further than broken promises.....

Or Lies you thought you wanted to hear.

Can heal truths you cannot bear.

Sometimes all we need and want is ....

Just a thought.

1 Hello, my name is Buttons

Parts of the Beginning

I am not sure where to begin. Mmm. Let me introduce myself. I am Buttons. I was born on a Monday, May 22, 1972 at 10:06am. Now I would like to believe I was born at 10:00am on the dot. Why? Because the doctor and nurses have to catch you; put you in the incubator; and then hand you to your mother. This process takes about 3-6 minutes. Because medical technology wasn't as advance in 1970s, I dear to say it took them 6 minutes, lol.

This was the year an African-American woman named Shirley Chisolm ran for President of the United States! The Civil Rights legislation was being implemented across America and minorities were getting their shot at the American Dream. The Vietnam War had just ended, and life was beginning to seem more hopeful. I would like to say I was born in the Year of Phenomenal Change!

Did you ever think about what happened on the day you were born? What the atmosphere was producing? I mean think about! What has influenced your existence? Take a moment and think about it. Look it up on Google! Research what happened the year you were born! (I'll wait for you if you want to stop now and look it up really quick, lol.)

Now back to what I was saying, I was born in the era of Phenomenal Change. Some of these stories are facts while others are more vague memories. The memories are mine as I recall them or from various sources like my father, mother, and sisters. For example, I will call my father, Rusty Jones (his street mechanic name), because I refuse to call him Dad. Rusty Jones was very abusive and an alcoholic. In 2014, I recall, Rusty Jones telling me at the age of two, I taught myself how to read by watching Sesame Street and Electric Company. I also loved Dr. Seuss books, because rhyming words was natural to me. I don't really remember, but that is what he told me. According to him I was a little genius.

Maybe I had to figure things out quickly, because he was an abusive alcoholic. I can believe I learned to read at about three, because I remember my daughter when she was three, sitting on the toilet reading Dr. Seuss', Green Eggs and Ham.

I do remember reading One Fish, Two Fish, Red Fish, Blue Fish lol! My mom said, I spent a great deal of time playing by myself. I liked to speak to my inner-self and create different worlds. It must run in the genes, lol.

I don't remember much about my childhood. It's more like flashes of different events. Some are good ones' other are lessons. Notice I didn't say "bad" ones. That's what Spiritual Law helps me understand. All experiences are lessons to learn. And my childhood was full of experiences. Moments that helped me heal emotionally, physically and spiritually. Each moment has allowed me to increase my understanding of myself. Setting me free from the traumatic events of my past. These traumas didn't happen overnight. Therefore, I am not going to heal overnight. I must take my time and be gentle.

As I talk to you through these pages. I'm struggling with not being able to deal with emotional stressors. I must tell myself, feelings are not facts, just feelings. It helps me to allow myself to feel the pain, while healing through my tears.

Allow me to share a memory with you. A time when I became a superhero. Parts of this recollection is from my actual memory and some is from conversations with Rusty Jones. This is the time when I became invincible. When I could defeat any bully, I encountered. Summoning my superhero is one of my many triggers. A trigger that has been both friend and foe.

A friend because it gives me the strength to overcome. But a foe, because at times I have an over-exaggerated ego of what I can accomplish. Through therapy I am learning the difference between the two. The first step was acknowledging that this memory can be used to help me today. It can be used to help me cope with my down days. Help rid myself of suicidal thoughts by calling on my strength and saying I will not let depression, PTSD, and anxiety defeat me. I will beat these bullies!

The Superhero is Born

Button's was playing outside the front yard in her favorite place, the mud! While creating Squirmy Mud Surprise Cakes and Hot Wheels trails, the neighborhood bullies began to walk her way. Button's never looked up, although she could sense her assailant. It was not enough of a danger, to signal Buttons to stop making her Hot Wheels drive on top of the moat.

One of the boys kicked dirt into her moat. The other pulled her pigtails. Buttons began to cry and ran into the house to tell Rusty Jones. As she ran, Buttons warned her assailants, "You better get out of here. I'm going to tell my Daddy and he is going to KILL YOU!"

Buttons swings open the screen door and yells for Rusty Jones, "Daddy! Daddy! The Belly Boys are picking on me!" To her astonishment, Buttons was not greeted with him swooping her up in his arms, gesture that always made her feel protected. No! She was faced with anger and disappointment. Rusty Jones handed Buttons a baseball bat. Her eyes opened wide. What does her Hero want a little girl like her to do with a bat? Rusty Jones sternly gave his marching orders, "You better go out there and bust them over the head with this bat until they bleed. I bet they won't mess with you again! You better not come in here crying, or else!" Buttons grabbed that bat and thought to herself, "Wow! I got superpowers too!" She walked towards the screen door and pushed it open with confidence. Right hand on the door. Left hand holding the bat. As the Belly Boys laughed the fearless five-year old superhero stepped forward daring them to come back. Little did they know her courage would conqueror them all.

"Hey, you want to pick on me now! I told you to leave me and my sisters ALONE!" The Belly Boys came running towards Buttons. She looked them in the eyes and one by one started swinging at their knee caps. Down they went. As Buttons was able to get the advantage she remembered her father's words, "Don't stop until they are bleeding!" The fear of disappointing her father and getting a spanking, gripped her. Buttons begins hitting each assailant in the nose until they bled. One by one they ran off.

Rusty Jones came outside and laughed. "Buttons, girl, you crazy! Nobody is ever gonna mess with you." Rusty Jones continued to chuckle. Buttons drops the bat and ran into her dad's arms. Squeezing Rusty Jones neck, she knows she's branded. THE NEW FAMILY SUPERHERO!

Like most little girls, I thought my dad was invincible. He could do no wrong. I remember a time when he was in a bad car accident. His stomach was split open and he was holding his guts in his hands when he came to the house door. I recall freaking out. But he told me not to worry as he left to walk to the hospital. The hospital was five miles away! That's my dad, my Superhero.

Often you will find me referencing myself as Buttons. That is my childhood character's name. Otherwise I will use "I" to describe myself as a teenager and as a woman. Throughout this writing I must continue to remind myself of the purpose. It's to tell the truth by peeling back the layers. Nothing like rigorous honesty to set your soul straight. Seriously, why keep it in? The only person whose is afraid of exposure is you. What if you weren't ashamed of your mistakes? Of your past choices? Of your looks? Of your mind? What if you loved you more than another person's opinion of you? What do you think would happen? Are you afraid to find out who you may really be? I was! I just recently, decided I was no longer going to live by other people's opinion or expectations of me.

Here's another little secret about me. There are times in my writing when you will notice me using seemingly inappropriate "lols". It's a defense mechanism. Sometimes I laugh at inappropriate times. You will also be a witness to my manic states. I am not going to hide myself in this personal dialogue. I want everyone to see the truth of what it is like to be highly intelligent while dealing with mental illness. You would never know it to look at me or through simple conversation, but I suffer from severe depression, post-traumatic stress disorder and severe anxiety. I went from being able to speak in front of thousands of people to cowering at the thought of being around a few. The anxiety has a profound physical effect on me. My hands jerk, while my head moves from side to side. It looks like I'm about to have a seizure. A lot of people experience some level of anxiety these days. How I got to a place of wanting to isolate is part of this journey. "What happened?"

I know we just started talking but please do me a favor? Take a moment and write down your name and address on an envelope. Then write down my publishing address. I would love for you to send me a letter. In it I want you to tell me what you are most afraid of? Or how you've overcame a great fear? I really want to know. Who knows maybe I'll share your story in my next book. This journey is about helping other. And you may be able to do just that. I hope you're enjoying our interaction so far? I want you to continue on this journey with me. There is, oh so much, for me to share. Hang on to your britches, because boy do I have a STORY to tell!

The Protector is Realized

This memory involves both of my parents. It happened on one of the many days Rusty Jones came home from work, drunk. These days usually entailed physical attack towards my Mom.

Buttons walks into the kitchen and her mom is cooking dinner. Rusty Jones hasn't come home from work yet. How does she know? Well, Buttons has been walking back and forth from the kitchen, where the backdoor is, to the living room, which is the front door entrance. Buttons stops in front of the stove. She looks up at her mother and reaches to touch her belly and say 'hello' to her unborn sister, when...

"Wanda, were you at? Woman if you don't get your ass out here!" Rusty Jones shouts from the living room. Buttons quickly pulls back her hand from her mom's now tense belly. Suddenly, she realizes, "I must protect them both now." Rusty Jones steps into the kitchen. He looks very angry and moves towards Buttons' mother. He raises his thick hand. Out the corner of her eye Buttons sees a butcher knife on the counter. She swiftly grabs it. Buttons bravely leaps forward while steadily pointing the knife at Rusty Jones' privates. "You hit my Mommy and I will cut it off," Buttons screamed directly at her father. Rusty Jones slowly lowered his hand, looking both amazed and afraid of his two and half year-old daughter, "Girl, you crazy!" Rusty Jones says while walking away. I have protected them both. "A knife could scare Daddy away," Buttons thought to herself. If I can stop Daddy. I can defeat ANYONE!"

This was the beginning of me becoming the "bully of all bullies", as my little sister would say. Oh! You should get a notebook or something and start writing down your thoughts. If you read something that makes you think about a moment in your life or you can just relate in some way, write it down now! Why? So, when I go on my book tour, you can bring your notebook for me to sign. I want to sign it where you realized something about yourself for the FIRST TIME. Remember if you take away labels and ages, you will see the character of a person. (Many people we encounter on our journey have the same characteristics. These are not learned behaviors. They are instinctual and personality traits. You encounter the same characters, different names, faces and backgrounds. But the same personality to teach you the lessons you need to learn from this life.)

Through my journey I have come to realize there are other ways God speaks to us. Numerology is understanding the nature of things through equations. Before I tell you more about this experience first let me say, I believe in numerology, (it's not Witchcraft or the Devils playground as Church Folk would have you believe). In numerology Three is a very significant number. A triangle has three sides and is difficult or impossible to break. Because of my beliefs I calculated the time from my great escape from Phi and the moment my spiritual connection occurred. It was exactly three weeks. Why is this important? It was a "hope shot" moment for me. It helped me to believe that I was not damaged goods.

One day I was talking to my sister on the phone leaving my last and final abuser. His name is Phi and I was engaged to him from February 2016 until May 12, 2016. I met him through mutual acquaintances when I lived in California in 2015. It was three weeks from when I left Phi, that I felt an overwhelming sensation of love and Warren's face popped into my mind's eye. It was sensational. I didn't kow I could feel love again. Especially after Phi physically and verbally attacked me as if he wanted to kill me!

Let me tell you! I've been in lovers' quarrels before, even with some tumbling around. Hell, Phi and I had a few tumbles. But this was different! Oh boy, was this different! It was like Phi never cared, loved, or was concerned for me. I wasn't human to him or even an animal. I was something Phi needed and wanted to destroy! I was bruised, battered and I ran. I called a friend. She sent me money to leave Nevada that same day. I packed what I could, and I headed to Ohio to my sister, Droopy Draws, house. When I arrived, she took a video of my body. I reached my sister's house at midnight, May 14, 2016, having driven non-stop from Nevada to Ohio! I stayed with my sister for ten days before I ventured home to Connecticut.

One person came to see me. It was Warren. I thought about Warren other than platonic. I wasn't even thinking about a relationship. That's why I was shocked that Warren's face popped up when I felt love. My soul deciding to connect itself to another human being was not of my will. I wasn't talking about Warren. I wasn't secretly thinking about him. But I needed to know I was loved by a man. Although the conversation with Droopy Draws wasn't about Warren or having a relationship. It was significant to me. It also changed the relationship Warren and I had.

Warren was an advocate for medical marijuana when I first met him. He suffered from the adverse effects of Lyme disease. He could barely walk without a cane. He used cannabis to ease his pain and help him have somewhat of a pain-free life. I was just starting out as an organizer on the issue. Warren was one of the many cannabis users who came to testify about changing the law to allow medicinal use of marijuana. I hadn't seen Warren in about three years before he came to visit me. I just returned to Connecticut and was staying with a friend. Warren came over and we talked for hours catching up on our lives. We talked about the Law of Attraction, spiritual connections, and yoga. I was grateful for his visit and his kindness. Before I forget, I was told that what happened on the phone that day wasn't a spiritual connection to Warren. It was my Kundalini rising! That's something you might want to YouTube or Google, lol.

I do believe in Devine intervention. I also believe we create our own life. What you consistently think on and speak about becomes your reality even if you are not aware of it happening. All I ever wanted was to love and be loved. However, God has a better plan for me. He wants me to be, LOVE! Now what does that mean? I don't really fully understand. But I am enjoying the journey though. I haven't a want or need for anything! All I have to do is BE. What is Love? Does anyone truly know? Perhaps I will discover it on this journey. What is love for you? Is it action or emotion? I don't know what real good love is so far. I am hoping to discover it.

When I left Phi on May 12, 2016, I left everything I just bought, including my inherited dish set Auntie Alicia left me prior to her death. I left my television, laptop and iPad, everything, even my painting of Ochun. I had a few clothes, some shoes, and MOST of my paperwork. I did make sure I had my spiritual artifacts. I need them to survive for real! lol My abuse by Phi is not the first time I was a victim. I was abused from childhood and periodically in my adult life. It would be real nice to know what love feels like. I felt it that day on the phone talking to Droopy Draws.

Let me say first, I love myself. It took a year and half to get to a place of self-love. I am focused on taking care of myself. I need to heal from 43 years of trauma and abuse. Most caused by others. The rest caused by me. The beginning of my abuse started at a young age. When your foundation is interrupted by sexual, mental, spiritual, and physical abuse, you are starting off in a deeper hole than most. I don't know if YOU, the reader will understand me. The impressions left on my young innocent mind has lasted beyond my own awareness of right and wrong. It has affected my personal and professional decision making. For example, why did I always have to be part of triangular relationships? Why I left the comforts of my own state to run to California? Why did I feel like no one will ever love ONLY me? How can I be LOVE, when what I know isn't love at all? I will share with you another painful memory. One that has left an impression of being comfortable in triangular relationships. Dealing with this memory helped me to understand why I was so comfortable being "the other woman" in many past relationships.

The "Other Woman" Syndrome

Buttons' Mom went to work as normal. She worked from 11pm – 7am. On this night Buttons' Mom came home earlier. Buttons was in her bed. Her sisters were sleep. It was now time for Rusty Jones and Buttons to have their "Special" time together. Rusty Jones was kneeling on the side of Buttons' bed. Her night gown was lifted, and he had his hands down her panties. It hurt, because Rusty Jones' hands were rough from working in the factory. Buttons inhaled deeply and didn't' say a word. She closed her eyes shut. "It will be over soon," Buttons said to herself.

Before she knew it, Buttons' mom was staring at her! Buttons lifted her head and said, "Hi Mommy! Daddy! Mommy is here now you can stop." Rusty Jones pulled his hand quickly away. Buttons mom looked at her with disgust. She stared Buttons down like she was the other woman! Through gritted teeth she yelled, "Buttons, get up and put on your shoes!" Buttons jumped out of the bed and put on her Skippy's. She ran to her mom's side. Buttons' mom nudged her away. Buttons stood close to her older sister Peaches. Buttons didn't know what she did wrong. Buttons thoughts raced through questions like, "Mommy knows Daddy does this to me all the time. We do it together. What's wrong this time?" Buttons mind went blank for a few seconds. Then she thought, "Why did Mommy look at me like that? She pushed me away like I was a bad girl." The feeling of shame overwhelmed her at the age of five. Buttons, her mom and sisters turned around and walked out the back door to the car. We left Rusty Jones behind and Buttons didn't understand why. Confused and sore, Buttons kept silent on the way to grandma's house.

I never recovered from this trauma. I am in a daily state of healing and understanding. Why do so many of my relationships end badly or in silence? I always felt like I no longer belonged to my family. My Mom's expression on her face that night continued to taunt me over the years. I was no longer her daughter, but her confidant, her competition. I was no longer her daughter, but the bitch who ruined her life. Oh yeah, there's more to this tragic story, smh!

My Mom slit her wrist in front of me when I was about nine or ten. As she cut into her skin she mumbled, "My life is fucked up because you exist!" How's that for your self-image? I wrote my mother a letter about being "The Other Woman" when I was twenty-five. I never gave it to her, but I will share it with you.

⌘

Dear Mom,

I am not the other woman! I am your child! I can recall when I was 12 years old and I had my first boyfriend. You walked around the house in that short blue robe, smelling like dead fish, and exposing your breast enough for a 15-year-old boy to get a hard on! I felt ashamed, embarrassed, and disrespected! I already was insecure, because I thought I was ugly and had little value. You figure you would make me seem more awkward and funny-looking. Just the fact that you said, I didn't have breast yet, was degrading. The sad thing was I did have some breast, they just weren't as big as yours! Lefty told me you tried to flirt with him. I believe you did it to get back at me. Oh! Let's not forget exposing yourself to Ben, who would love to have sex with you? Why? I don't know, but he told me that on several occasions when he lived with us. You even took him with you to Delores' house to smoke weed and have orgies! Once again you thought you won! You said that you didn't blame me for what Rusty Jones did. You lied to me and to yourself for years because every chance you had, you tried to steal my boyfriends by flaunting sex in front of them! That's something I use to do years ago!

Instead of talking about me, my dreams and goals in life, when I met someone. I talked about how great I was in bed. When I did get the man or woman I never thought they would actually love me for me. Why? Because I offered sex and I believed that's all I was good for! How could you try and make me out to be your adversary? I am your daughter! For years I just wanted you to love me and not abuse me in anyway. For years I thought I was crazy because you were so convincing when you said something didn't happen, when it REALLY did!

Even with my children's fathers you tested to see who was better as a mother! You always compare my parenting to yours. When will it end? When will you see me as your daughter and not the other woman? I never tried to hurt you. I never wanted <u>any</u> of **your** *men!!! You always wanted mine. You used men for your own sick personal agenda. Then discard them like trash! Just like you use to do me. You know I don't like asking any man that's not a relative for money. I don't care if he said he was madly in-love with me and wants me to have all 10 of his children! I don't like depending or asking a man for anything financially. You also know, that for you I would ask a man for money to repay him back, because YOU WON'T! It was my first date with Scuffy, Budda's father. We met 2 days before that date. I was so excited. He didn't want sex Ma! He wanted to talk to me. Guess what? I had nothing important to say about myself, except how good I was in bed! Oh yeah, I mentioned my poems. Then I began to prostitute myself just like I saw you do for years. The same way you accused me of doing when I was a child and a teenager. Well Ma, for you on that first date with Scuffy I asked for the $50, so you could go home! I'm supposed to ask YOU for money, in case he turned out to be some psychopath and I needed a cab home! You know what? I had* *sex with him that night to pay him back that $50! I knew you wouldn't! That's one in many situations. I used to think it was just all in my head. Until I was in jail.*

Whenever I introduced you to a female partner you flirted with them. You told one person that I was a scared little girl and I would never really be able to satisfy anyone in bed. I am not having a sex war with you mother. This is not about who's better in bed and that's why they stay or leave. This is not a competition to see who can have the best relationships and who's a better mother! You always wondered what made me so special and different from you, Peaches and Droopy Drawers! It's something you all consider a weakness. I care about people's feelings, and how they feel about themselves. That's it! Not my body, brain or my bedroom techniques. It's my nature to care for the next person, because I care enough about me!

If I really sat down and think good and long. I have loved myself through the worst years of my life. I gave myself personal vacations and behaved like a kid for a few days every now and then. I learned to give myself foot messages and made treats for me. When things got really bad I would go to the park or by a brook to cry to God. Because I couldn't cry to you. Almost 20 years later and I'm still crying to God. The best part about now compared to then is, I know God loves me and He hears me. He even helps me without obligations or strings attached. I love me today, Ma! No matter what I've done, I'm forgiven. I give myself permission to receive that forgiveness from God and from myself. I didn't take away your men or take up your time. I was a little girl without a Dad and listened to the men that told me how much they loved my mother. I listened! I never cast a spell or try to lure them with my boyish figure. We just all had something in common and gave each other hope... We loved you and couldn't figure out why you couldn't love us back. Today I know a reason and there are probably a few more. One is because you couldn't love yourself.

It's sad Mom that you thought this little girl could ever take away all the men in your life. Even your only son. I didn't nor did I ever want to! It hurts to know I was your child and all you saw was the other woman. You couldn't love me as your daughter anymore, so you made me your friend! I don't want to be your friend! I want to be your child! I don't want to be the other woman. I'm NOT the one who took your men! I am your daughter!

As I come to the end, the tears have stopped flowing down my face. The pain in the center of my being is gone and I feel refreshed and free. I finally got a chance to say how I really feel about the way you treated me without feeling guilty, bad, ashamed or wanting to clean it up! I don't have to fix it! That is not why I was born! You treated me like shit then you dressed it up with some good words. Words that have become taboo to me. You would say I was 'special' or 'different'. You would tell me you loved me more than the others, because you are special or different, or you've got something others wish they had! All are good things to say to a child, teenager, adult and should boost their esteem. However, you used them to abuse me and torment me! FUCK YOU and your poor choice of words! They won't hurt me anymore! I won't let you or them. Guess what you lose after all. I always wanted to tell you that! I always wanted to say, "FUCK YOU!" without feeling bad or guilty, because you are my mother. Worried about other people's opinions. Well, fuck them too! Damn that feels good! I'm a little freer and a lot more healthier! Amen

⌘

I know the letter is harsh. It's especially hard to read if you had a great mom, someone who loved and protected you. I just know it was necessary to try to heal this old wound. So, many people ask me why I don't see my value and beauty. Tell me how you can think of yourself as valuable, when your OWN MOTHER rejects you? You can with therapy and several crashed relationships, you too can learn to love and value yourself. It's a daily struggle at times. There are days I can look in the mirror see my beauty and walk away forgetting the image I just saw. When I drive down the street, I sometimes get a glimpse of myself in the rear-view mirror. I have beautiful brown eyes lol. That's when I remember I am beautiful. I believe beauty is relative to how you feel about yourself. When I feel bad on the inside I recite, 'Phenomenal Woman' by Dr. Maya Angelou. When I need to feel my own love for self, I place my right hand over my heart and say, "I love you, Buttons." These three things help me with my self-image and promotes self-love. Now I must confess. I too need to hear from others that I have value. Not for attention. I need it to validate my existence. Why? Because I do. It helps. Let me give you an example.

On Sunday, June 19, 2016, I wrote on Facebook that I had unwanted emotions because of unwarranted thoughts. I felt bad enough that I wanted to kill myself! OMG! How could I even conceive such a thing? This is part of living with severe depression with PTSD. I thought I processed the rejection and abandonment feelings I felt from days ago. I thought I knew it wasn't my fault or anything I did that caused Warren to treat me with disrespect. I thought my tears that were shed were sufficient. They were NOT! Because feelings of rejection and abandonment are deep wounds in my soul. A few tears weren't enough to move on. So, what happened to bring on these negative feelings? It's simple, Warren turns out, wasn't ready to move beyond his abusive ex-girlfriend. She called him Tuesday, June 14, 2016 demanding Warren to mail her items, belongings, SHIT to her. Warren called me and said, "My heart is still connected to her. How can I move forward until I close this chapter of my life?" Nice right? WRONG! I thought it was nice at first too. Until I realized that it was a scapegoat. I just spent the best five days and four nights I had in a long time. I never had an experience like it before. It was wonderful.

Warren spoke to me with respect and kindness. He held my hand to let me know everything was going to work out okay. When I got upset he didn't just dismiss it or diminish my feelings. When I started to cry about an invasive thought or talked about my abuse. Warren immediately held me in his arms. We woke up and meditated and practiced Tribal Yoga positions. I felt safe. I felt understood. I felt.... well I felt LOVED. At least what I imagined love to feel like. Then it all went away, smh.

That Thursday, I went to Warren's house just to be near him. To feel his energy. Within a few hours of being there Warren tells me I'm making him anxious, just by being in his house and taking a nap in his bed. I thought I was helping by staying out of his way and taking the dogs with me. Yes, Warren has two great dogs. I was connected to them too. It's like I went from Heaven to Hell in a matter of a week! What happened to staying in the moment and letting our souls guide us? What happened to, "This is the best I felt ever!" Lesson learned! It doesn't matter how nice someone brushes you off. Rejection is still rejection! Then on Friday morning, June 17th, 2016, Roy told me not to come visit him. Two rejections in twenty-four hours! I was broken on the inside.

Who is Roy? Roy is my friend, who is incarcerated. We became friends because I can relate to being incarcerated and the value of human contact. Even if it's just sitting and talking to someone face-to-face for a few hours a week. Now, I have a set day when I visit Roy. It's every Friday. On this particular Friday, an old friend of his decided she wanted to visit Roy. She hadn't spoken to him for almost a year. Now Roy had no idea what happened to me on Thursday afternoon. Nor did Roy know I was already feeling rejected and needed a friend to talk to about Warren. My first response was "okay" she finally came around. My second thought, well it was a dozy, lol. I immediately took it in a whole different direction. First, I thought, "Is he trying to act like me and him is an item or something?" Then I went to, "How could he do this to me!" My final stage was, "I am overreacting, and I just need to be frank and ask him." Emails and texts do not give way to emotional context. What Roy wanted was a few hours with his friend to talk about WHY she hasn't communicated with him for a year. Well, when your emotions are all over the place in the negative sphere. You instantly think negative about EVERYTHING! Funny how the brain works that way. So, now I felt rejected and abandon, lol!

My subconscious was not done dealing with my rejection and abandonment emotions. I was facing the same emotional turmoil I felt as child, now in an adult situation. Hence, the childish response or should I say, "Childish Reactions". These feelings are illogical to me. I don't

19

understand them, yet I feel this deep sadness that hurts my very essences. This pain at times is so overwhelming that I just want it to STOP! In my emotional state the only way out, I could think of was DEATH. I knew from my recent experience on March 17, 2016, that killing myself was not an option. So, I went to a church and prayed on the steps. Then I went to the beach.

Phi was my fiancée. We got engaged in February 2016. Phi and I had left Los Angeles and moved to Nevada. We were friends. When I was first diagnosed with Post Traumatic Stress Disorder, depression and anxiety. Phi was there for me. I couldn't even leave my bedroom. We talked. Phi was the one who told me Zoloft was making me more depressed. He took my pills and flushed them down the toilet. He stayed with me for about a week. I felt a little better. Phi then convinced me to go outside for a walk. At that time, I hadn't been outside for two months. I went to the doctor, but that was it. Because of this I thought I could trust Phi with my life. That was until March 17, 2016. It was my last attempt at suicide.

What happened on St. Patrick's Day 2016? Well, I took all of my Ativan and Risperidone, both are psych medications. I was in a comma for three days. Mind you, Phi never called the police, ambulance or anything. He just made sure I was breathing. I slept for three whole freakin' days! Ugh! SMMFH! After I woke up. I asked Phi how long I was asleep. He said three days. I didn't say anything. As I walked to the bathroom from the bedroom. I knew not to try to take my own life again, and to get around positive spiritual people. So, I went to church. The message came from 2 Samuel chapter 9, 'God is looking for you, while you are in a low place and crippled. Of course, I said, "That's Me!!!" I was low in spirit and crippled in my mind. I paid close attention to the message. If I put God in the position of David, then that means God is sending His Angels to take charge/protection over me. That God wants to bless me and put me up on high. I will eat at God's table continuously! Of course, I latch on to that concept and it carried me through the negative thoughts.

Your thoughts become your actions if you do not check your thoughts and emotions. Sometimes you can think something so terrible that it happens to you regularly. So much so, that you cannot think of a way out or have hope. My wish is that this journey gives you hope. Despite your situation and circumstance, you can find enough light inside of you to HOPE, WANT, DESIRE, and SPEAK IT into existence everything that is GOOD. Or you can remain negative and negativity will keep coming! I will give you two examples. One will be what substance use disorder counselors and participants call, "Stinkin' Thinkin'." The other is what those from the world of Law of Attraction called "Positive Thought Manifest Positive Results".

My 'RAPE ME' Stamp

My mom had a boyfriend named Richard, when I was about 8 or 9 years old. Richard like Rusty Jones is a pedophile. Kind of makes me wonder about my Mom's attraction meter. Mmm. What Richard did cause me to believe I was branded for life.

It was a nice day out. The sun was shining, and the sky was blue. It was warm, and children were playing outside. The window was open, and you can hear the laughter of the young. Buttons and her sisters wanted to go outside and play. Richard was babysitting. Buttons and her sisters walked out the bedroom headed for the door. They stopped. Buttons had to use the bathroom. When she came out of the bathroom, Richard had Peaches pinned down on the couch trying to snatch her bottoms off. "Droopy Drawers hide in the bathroom," Buttons whispered, while she grabbed a whiffle ball bat. Buttons ran into the living room and began swinging on Richard's back demanding he release Peaches. Peaches escaped, and Buttons yelled, "Take the phone and hide with Droopy Drawers in the bathroom. Call the police!" Richard grabbed Buttons by the throat and slammed her on the couch. He had Buttons underneath him! The bat laid on the side of the couch. Buttons face was stinging from his slap. She didn't cry. Squirming she first screamed for her sisters to help. Then Buttons went numb. For what seemed like an hour, Buttons watched her eight-year-old body being raped. Buttons blacked out.

A month or two later, Buttons had cramps in school that were so severe, she went to the school nurse. The nurse told her to use the toilet. Buttons sat on the toilet and a big blood clot came out! Buttons was scared but didn't yell for help. Somehow, she knew something was wrong. It was her first and only miscarriage.

I didn't know I was having a miscarriage, at the time. I don't remember what happened after Richard finished molesting me. I just knew that from now on I was damaged goods and people can just rape me at their leisure. Every five years from that point on I got raped. I believed I had a stamp across my forehead that said, "RAPE ME!" The negative energy of that subconscious thought drew abusers to me. I got raped every five years like clockwork. I drew to me abusers that said, "I love you," then turned around and raped me or I just met someone I thought was nice that on our first date raped me.

21

Then there was Ben. Ben mentally, emotionally, and sexually assaulted me on a regular basis. I thought it was love. I used to brag about being a wife at thirteen in the 8th grade. You see Ben was eighteen during this time. My mom allowed him to live with us. I looked back on this time with mixed feelings. Being a mother now myself, I would've choked the Hell out of an eighteen-year-old trying to be my thirteen year old daughter's boyfriend! Then there is the harsh reality of that time in my life. I needed Ben to love me. I needed someone to care enough about me, because my Mom didn't. To her I was always the 'Other Woman' in her life. Smh

Writing through the tears, all I ever wanted was my mother's love. I thought I was helping my parents with their sex life. I didn't understand what I did wrong to have my mother treat me like.... SHIT! It hurts still. Yes, even though I have forgiven my parents, the pain knows not forgiveness. It just knows pain. This pain was never grieved away. My younger self will never know what it was like to have a loving, caring, nurturing mother. I will never know what it's like to cry on my mother's shoulder. Instead I ALWAYS had to be the strong one. And I was! My mom knew I was resilient as a child. She knew I was stronger than them all. That brings me to my Positive Thoughts, Positive Results story.

Meeting Dr. Maya Angelou

I walk into the Legislative Office Building heading towards the Capitol. I am a community organizer, advocate, and community lobbyist. I was working on several pieces of legislation. I head over to meet my good friend, Grace. Grace's desk is right in front as soon as you walk through the door. Grace was extra excited to see me. She asked me to step into the hallway.

We are both believers in God/Yaweh/Jesus/Elohim/Holy Spirit/Yashua, so I am ready to shout at her praise report. So, now I am doing the two-step anxiously waiting for the GOOD NEWS! Grace starts off by asking me if I knew Maya Angelou was coming to the Bushnell. I said, 'Yes, girl and I already have my front row ticket!" I wasn't going to miss another opportunity to see Dr. Angelou in the flesh!" Grace's head went down. She paused and started to speak slow and low. I got closer to her. I asked her if she was alright. Grace looked up at me and said, "Remember when you came to speak to my teen girls' group?" I nodded yes. "Remember you recited Phenomenal Woman and told the girls about being raped in prison? How that poem gave you inner strength to leave your roommate, who was also your abuser?" I said, "Yes. What's up?"

Grace continued, her eyes were starting to water. I got closer. She says, "These are tears of joy!" I felt relieved. I had on my shouting shoes, so I was ready when she was! Grace grabbed my hands and looked into my eyes. "What I remember most was your faith. You said, 'When I meet Maya Angelou. I am going to tell her how her poem saved my life when I was in a dark place.' You said, "When." I was like "YES, WHEN!" Now I am nervous and a little emotional. I wasn't sure what she was going to say next. "Lord, if Maya Angelou comes out of that office door I am going to faint," I thought to myself.

Grace tells me about her friend working at the Bushnell organizing Dr. Angelou's upcoming event. I was excited because I had already bought 2 tickets and asked my friend Janet to come with me. I'm thinking we can make it a "Women's Night Out!" Then Grace hits me with an email exchange between her, her friend and Dr. Angelou's assistant. I asked, "What is this?" Grace holds my hands again. "It is my pleasure to tell you that this week you will finally meet Dr. Maya Angelou in person! I got you two backstage passes! If you didn't have tickets I had that on hold for you too!" My face lit up, "Girrrrrrrrrrl!!!! God is too good to me! Hallelujah, Hallelujah!! I'm going to meet her?! You are lying, girl I cannot believe it!" We stood in the hallway, shouting up a storm! We didn't care who saw us. We stood dancing for the Lord about five minutes. Then it really sunk in. I am going to FINALLY meet the woman who saved me with her words.

(Flashback) I am 25 years old, in prison, roommates with my rapist, and on trial facing twenty to life imprisonment for defending my children and my own life. My roommate was the woman who raped me for almost eight months. She made me her bitch! I pretended to love her out of survival. Most people thought we were a happy couple.

To survive, I had convinced myself I loved Papa, as the women in prison called her. Something I am all too familiar with...lying to myself about my real-life situation to make it through. (Flashback Over)

Question, do you lie to yourself? Do you fabricate your current situation to stay with someone who is abusive or mistreats you? I challenge you to write down the truth of your current relationships. It doesn't have to be a lover or partner. It can be a co-worker or a family member. Just be honest about it. Remember to write the truth and make a positive decision based on that truth. Once you write it down, read it and then burn it.

Now back to meeting Maya Angelou. I stopped shouting and started crying! Flashes of days practicing Phenomenal Woman came back to me like a flood. I remembered practicing each hand gesture and body movement that went with the words...*Pretty women wonder were my secret lies. I'm not cute or built to suit a fashion model size*...yes, ever arm motion, every step, every word, I remembered and recited. Wow! I was finally meeting her! I began to recall the evening in that class, Overcoming Obstacles. When I recited it and became...Phenomenal Woman! I hugged Grace so hard, I thought I would break her, lol.

The night with Maya Angelou came. I picked up my frined Janet. I was so excited. After all this time of knowing, believing, and hoping. I am only moments away of meeting her, touching her, hugging her even. I walk into a back room. I had to pass a few grey lockers I guess artist use when they perform. I turn the corner. "YOU ARE GEORGEOUS!" Did Maya Angelou say I was gorgeous? Okay world forget your thoughts about my beauty. Dr. Maya Angelou said I was gorgeous! The tears immediately began to flow. I introduced her to Janet. Then I began to tell her my story about being on trial, living with a woman who raped me in jail. Dr. Angelou stopped me mid-story. "I know your story Buttons. I want you to know something." I stood closer to her. She grabbed my hand. "I'm leaning on you. So, stand tall! When you can't do anything else, just STAND! Know, that I am there leaning on you in support. So, stand and don't let anyone or anything move you." I hugged and kissed her. Janet and I took pictures. Who knew after all this time my story touched Dr. Angelou so much it gave her strength. I walked out of that room feeling...I cannot put it in words. How would you feel if your life saving hero told you, they were leaning on you?

That very poem on my worst days still can pick me up out of a funk. Sometimes it's the phrase, *"Men themselves wonder what they see in me. They try so much, but they can't touch my inner mystery."* I remembered on the night I first recited the poem, after practicing for a week. I promised everyone that I would meet Dr. Maya Angelou one day. Yes, I was in prison facing twenty years or more and knew that God would allow me to meet this amazing woman, who gave me courage, an image I can believe in for myself. There was never any doubt. This is the hope that I spoke of earlier on. It took sixteen years after receiving Phenomenal Woman before I met her. But it happened nonetheless. Some treasures or life altering events take a little longer than others. The reckoning is that they really do happen.

I was on the phone the day Dr. Maya Angelou died. It was her last and final interview. Who knew, but God! I was blessed to meet her and further blessed to be on that last historic interview she had with asha bandele.

How's that for positive thinking? You can create your world. Don't let the world create you. The minute you do, you're lost. You lose YOU! Let me put it in personal terms. When I allowed the world to create me, I got lost. I got so lost, one day I finally broke. I hurt from my core. I couldn't remember why I existed. It seemed like nothing could get me out of this cloud of depression. I had lost my job, because of my chronic PTSD with psychosomatic seizures. I lost my apartment. And I finally, I thought, I lost my mind. That's when I fell away from faith in God. How you ask? Well let me tell you. Being positive around vampire soul-sucking leeches, can cause you a great deal of pain. Especially if you are the one who is doing more giving than receiving. I thought, "If God is so loving. Why did He let me lose EVERYTHING? Where was He now in my darkest hour?" I lost sight of my purpose and why I existed.

Dr. Maya Angelou and Me at Hartford Bushnell Theater

25

LARESSE HARVEY

The Middle Collides with The End of The Beginning

A week before Thanksgiving 2012, I was 40 years old, I called my Mom to say I was sorry for being such a bitch towards her. I was thinking that perhaps my reoccurring nightmares were somehow false. I wanted to stop hating my Mom for whatever, she had done. The phone call went like this,

Me: "Mom, I am so sorry for treating you bad. Can you please forgive me? I just...."

Mom: *Interrupting me,* "No, no, Buttons. I need you to forgive me for what your father and I did to you. I used to call you to our bedroom. I would whisper in your ear to be very quiet and still. That you were helping your dad and me. I would tell you that you were special and a good girl, because you were saving our family

Me: "Mommy, thank you for telling me the truth." *Feelings of relief flooded my body. I wasn't crazy! My memories are REAL! Whew.* "Mommy it's okay. I forgive you. I know you were being abused too. Why ME?"

Mom: *Sigh.* "Because you were stronger than me. I needed someone to blame. I blamed you. I am so sorry Buttons. You are still stronger than your sisters and me. I am so sorry."

Me: Tears streaming down my face. "It's okay Mom. I love you. I have to hang up now."

Mom: "I love you baby. Let's talk again real soon, okay?"

Me: "Okay, Mom. Bye."

I immediately, fell to my knees and thanked God for setting me free! I cried for the little girl, who didn't know she was a pawn in a grown woman's survival tactics. I cried for the grown woman, who finally understood her desperation to belong to someone and be loved. I cried for my mother, who had to live with the guilt and shame of turning on her child. You know that cry that is silent, but your mouth is wide open and comes from the pit of your stomach? I cried liked that for about fifteen minutes. Then I got up and started praising God! I told myself that is enough tears. Now get a therapist and recover! That's exactly what I did. I went to the local YWCA and weekly met with a Sexual Assault Crisis counselor. I began to unravel my decisions in men, relationship triangles,

26

and my own need to be accepted and loved.

Funny thing about getting mentally healthy, people who are around you begin to act out. It made me second guess myself at times. Then something clicked. Those people are acting out, because you are NOT THE SAME. The manipulation techniques no longer hold. The ability to push my buttons and make me "act right" no longer worked in the same way.

I began to see how I was my own abuser by keeping myself in a comfort zone of familiarity. It's not pleasant facing yourself, while working on deeply rooted character flaws. It's very difficult to admit that the one thing you've been searching for in your love life is a man like your abusive father. Twisted? Not really.

What I missed was the father that was the superhero. The attention Rusty Jones gave me. I missed fixing on cars or taking all his friends money at the pool hall. I was a pool-shark at five years old, lol. It was one of my favorite things I did with Rusty Jones. We would go and pretend I couldn't play billiards. I missed belonging to a man. I missed it so much, that I would be with any fella that said I was pretty. It didn't take much seduction or effort on a man's part. Mmm. I still do that shit! If I am honest with myself, that's how I fell for Q, Phi, Warren and my ex-husband! I'm still searching to belong to a man.

I want a healthy loving, kind, understanding man. Not another manipulator of any kind. I know he exists. There is SOMEONE for EVERYONE! I just haven't found that someone. I haven't given up hope. I just hope that when we find each other there is more than just a few days, years, or months. I pray we have each other for twenty plus years! Yahweh-Yashua needs to get on that expeditiously! I am forty-four years old, lol. Whenever it happens, I am positive the time my Soulmate and I share will be more than enough. Love knows no bounds and can heal even the deepest wounds of the soul. I will remain optimistic.

Well my three and half hour classical music has ended. Therefore, my day of writing has ended too. Tomorrow is Friday, July 1, 2016. I go to visit Roy and then back to writing. I am enjoying this conversation with you. I hope you are starting to know me a little better now. Yes, I'm serious about you taking notes to write to me. You can ask me anything! Well anything, except the real names of people, lol. Until tomorrow. Keep positive! Keep Optimistic! KEEP HOPING FOR BETTER! Whatever your BETTER is, keep it in the front and back of your mind. Whatever you dwell on, that becomes your reality.

Public Enemy #1

Today is July 1, 2016, it is exactly the middle of the year! Yes, 168 days gone 168 days to go! I am breaking negative cycles of abuse and trauma daily. I had an interesting conversation with Warren today. He was telling me that he wants to talk to me, but it is a conversation not to be had over the phone. It got me thinking. Is he trying to remove all of his connections with his ex-girlfriend to be with me? Wow! If that is true, then I missed judged him completely! We will see how it all works out! Won't WE?! It reminded me of an argument I had with my daughter. The day we stopped being Mother and Daughter. The day I damn near beat her to death without prejudice. The day I became Public Enemy number one!

Sometime in September 2001, MaMa, my nickname for my daughter, was 14 years old and a freshman at New Britain High School. I am a 29-year-old newlywed, trying to help my husband get his funeral home on track, and keep my sanity. I've been home from prison for almost two years. Mama has called everyone she knew to take her in and let her live with them. I guess living with me was too hard for her. Mama didn't care how I felt. All she wanted was to maintain the social status she became accustomed to...being a victim of circumstance.

On this day Mama realizes no one will allow her to move in, because I was home from prison. More importantly, because I was her mother. I believe it was at this moment, Mama internalized, "Being with Mommy makes me the black sheep too! Mommy is the ENEMY!"

"Mama what is wrong with you?" I asked. "I don't want to live with you! I want to live with my Dad!" she replied screaming. Mama is in full challenging authority mode. "Listen, you can call whoever you want. I am home now, and you live with me. No one is going to take you! Get it through your head! You ARE MY DAUGHTER! I HAD YOU! NO ONE ELSE! ME!" I pound on my chest to prove that I am serious. Mama slams the door to her bedroom screaming, "I HATE YOU! GO BACK TO JAIL! I DON'T WANT TO LIVE WITH YOU! I HATE YOU!" I busted open the door and like a crazed maniac I pounced on my daughter and began beating the shit out of her. I was so angry and hurt! I couldn't believe this selfish bitch wanted me back in jail! Did she even know what emotional distress I was in while there? No, she is a fourteen year old spoiled brat and I'm going to beat that bullshit out of her! I don't know how long I hit her or if I did it with open hand or a belt? What I do remember was hearing her whimper. I totally blacked out. Every painful and unjust experience I went through in jail to save her life rushed through me. I felt like she was ungrateful. "I got raped by woman because I protected you!" I shouted as I hit her. I stood trial facing 20 years to life! That was another hit. I lost my soul and innocence to give you life! And another! The hits kept coming as the anger kept boiling up. I was remembering the pain I suffered. "Mama you get your ass up and clean this room! Nobody wants you because I am here! I always wanted you! They feel obligated not love! If they loved, you SOMEONE WOULD WANT YOUR DUMBASS BESIDES ME!" "Grandma loves me! I don't care! I hate you!" Mama shouted. I looked at her. That moment I knew this is the end of our Mother/Daughter relationship. It ended 14 years ago. I'm just facing it now. I will never be her mother. Just the woman that gave birth to her. I will never be good or great enough. Nor do I hope to be, or do I?

I used to try and make myself the image of a woman that was suitable for my children. I had to realize that they want to play victim to my prison sentence. I was in prison for six years. Now I am paying a lifetime sentence of never being my children's Mother.

In time I hope my children and I can have a relationship that others envy. What better way to show others that a love between mother and child can withstand the harshest realities of the past. A conviction doesn't just punish the defendant or accused. It punishes families. What if judges and prosecutors took that into consideration before sentencing people? What if people didn't judge the children because their parents made a mistake? It should be easier for a parent to have contact visits often with their child(ren). What if?

Visiting Roy

My visits with Roy are always refreshing. Roy doesn't judge me or my actions. I told Roy about why I went to the hospital on Sunday, June 26, 2016. We laughed at my little excursion with Candy! What had happened was...Candy's brother hit her over the head with a brown paper bag. Did I mention that had two 22-ounce cans of beer in it? Why did he hit her? Because she kicked him out of the car for being rude, disrespectful and among other things high as a kite! Well, he tried to hit Candy again. I immediately jumped out of the driver's seat and pushed him away from Candy. I jumped back in the car and slowly pulled off in reverse. Candy's brother jumped up and pour beer all over her and hit her in the head with the can! We drove to the end of the dirt road to tell the female officer, who was parked there what happened. Candy's brother was arrested within twenty minutes for having paraphernalia. Candy put a Protective Order against him. Thank the Lord!

Candy's brother is one of the "Tent People" this town calls their homeless. I will keep my opinion to myself. It just amazes me how affluent communities try to hide their dysfunctions from the world. Do they not understand that what's done in the dark will eventually come to the LIGHT? I mean there are kids dying of overdose deaths in this town. You know the old saying, "Not in my backyard!" Well their backyard is spilling over to the front and their filth is showing! This doesn't just happen in communities of color or impoverished communities. The only REAL difference is most urban communities can't COVER IT UP WITH MONEY! I digress. Forgive my outburst. It's painful to know that people no matter what color are treated like animals.

Of course, the incident traumatized me, and I started to have psychosomatic-seizures later that day. I rested Friday and all-day Saturday. Late Saturday evening my left arm went numb. On Sunday morning there was only a little feeling in my left arm and my chest was tight. Candy took me to the emergency room. As soon as I walked up to the front desk to check in I started to have psychosomatic seizures again! I was taken to the back and put in a room. The doctor asked me to stop shaking! I was like, "This Bitch is about to get her feelings hurt! If I could stop shaking I would!" Excuse my vulgar language. It's the truth though, lol! I said, "I can't! If I could, I would," through greeted teeth, because I was still seizing! Of course, we all know the diagnosis...Chronic PTSD. The best thing was I got a CAT scan of my brain. Everything looked normal. So, the doctor referred me to a psychiatrist in town. Her statement to me was, "Maybe you weren't getting the correct type of therapy for your extensive trauma in California."

I had hoped the doctor's recommendation would help more than the therapy I'd been receiving. The other part to that is...how does she know? Really? While going to therapy in California I was being abused without realizing it. So, how does she know the therapy I was receiving wasn't helpful? It helped me see what was at the root of my psychosomatic seizures. Well we will see if she was right. Now back to Roy, lol!

Roy and I chuckled over the incident with Candy's brother. Yes, it was a serious situation. Roy and I continued our visit talking about what he plans to do when he gets released.

Sometimes I choose to use humor to overcome difficult times. Other times I simply choose to forget. In forgetting the past, I have lost a lot time and teachable moments of my youth, teenage and adult life. Like moments of abuse or even positive events! When abuse happened to me I would instantly forgive and forget. Even when a person traumatized me repeatedly. I behaved as if it happened for the first time. Why? Because I genuinely forgot about the first and any other time after that. It's a defense mechanism. Now I use meditation to recall my past and to keep calm. I must admit I don't meditate daily. Sometimes meditation causes me to have my seizures. I do try and meditate once a week.

Do you meditate? Do you even know how? Well, if you do meditate you are ahead of the game. Part of manifesting your positive life is visualizing it. Meditation helps get your mind focused, so you can weed out the negative and keep all the positive. Let's do a quick breathing meditation!

We will take 12 deep breathes in total. Sit with your spine straight or lay flat. Tense up your whole body, so you can feel the difference when you are relaxed. You will first do what is called a Cleansing breath. You inhale through the nose, while keeping your tongue to the roof of your mouth. Exhale out your mouth, relaxing your tongue. The other 9 breathes are in and out the nose for a count of five inhale in; hold for a count of three exhale for a count of five. While breathing through the nose and exhaling keep your tongue at the roof of your mouth. Don't focus on any thought. If something comes up refocus back on counting your breathes. At the end keep your eyes close for a few moments, while you go back to breathing normally. You got the instructions? Alright, let's go!

Brief Meditation: Focus on Breathing

Siting or laying down: Tense your whole body, including your feet, while taking in the Cleansing Breath.

Exhale and relax your body. Take another Cleansing Breath without tensing your body.

Hands flat on your knees or on the side. Take the first of the 9 breathes through your nose for a count of 5. Hold for a count of 3. Release through the mouth for a count of 5.

Breathe number 2 inhale through your nose for a count of 5. Hold for a count of 3. Exhale through your mouth for a count of 5. Repeat.

Breath number 3 inhale through your nose for a count of 5. Hold for a count of 3. Exhale through your mouth for a count of 5. Repeat.

Breathe number 4 inhale through your nose for a count of 5. Hold for a count of 3. Exhale through your mouth for a count of 5. Repeat.

Breathe number 5 inhale through your nose for a count of 5. Hold for a count of 3. Exhale through your mouth for a count of 5. Repeat.

You are doing great! Keep going! Only four more breathes to go!

Breathe number 6 and 7 inhale through your nose for a count of 5. Hold for a count of 3. Exhale through your mouth for a count of 5. Repeat.

Breath number 8 inhale through your nose for a count of 5. Hold for a count of 3. Exhale through your mouth for a count of 5. Repeat.

Last ONE inhale through your nose for a count of 5. Hold for a count of 3. Exhale through your mouth for a count of 5.

Last breathe is a Cleansing Breathe... Breath in through your nose. Exhale out your mouth. Keep your eyes close and feel what's going on in your body. ***Concentrate on the Sri Yantra (image below). It should help!***

What thoughts came up? Did you feel a tingling sensation? Did a nagging question become clear? Perhaps, nothing happened except you got to relax for 4 minutes!

Once you get the breathing down, then you can focus on various energy sources of the body called Chakras! I am not an expert on the subject, yet. I do know opening my third-eye and getting my Chakras cleanse did help me grow spiritually. It also allowed me to see where I was hurting; how to dump negative energy; and find myself! For years I thought my life's purpose was to take care of those who couldn't fight or speak for themselves. Like Droopy Drawers said, "I was the Bully of the Bullies." I didn't bully the bullies. I just confronted them and occasionally, beat them up for picking on other kids, youth, young adults, adults, and elderly. But I could never see or fight against my own bullies. Funny how that works. Through meditation and some crafty yoga stand, I found my true life's purpose! I will say this to you. I had to have the life experiences and training in order to fulfill my purpose. I hope that by beginning a daily Breathing Meditation you will find yourself as I am finding myself!

No Labels Please!

I want to talk to you about beating statistics. Just because you fall into a category, don't let society brand you. I was a teen-mom. I got pregnant at fourteen and had my first child at fifteen. I had her because I wanted someone to love me unconditionally. Funny thing about that is, children grow up to be people too! They grow up and then family, friends, and society, helps them to put conditions on their love for you. Going to prison for six years didn't help either!

At fifteen I was attending my sophomore year of high school. I was part of a group of teenage mothers, who spoke around the state of Connecticut, about the dangers of unprotected sex and the downfalls of being a teen-mom. My daughter was born in October of 1987. In 1988 I was in Washington, D.C., staying at the same hotel former president Ronald Reagan was shot. There was a small pool with a Grand Piano in the center of it. A handsome White gentleman was playing Johann Sebastian Bach's Sinfonia in F-minor. Of course, I went on YouTube to make sure I wrote the music down correctly, lol. It reminded me of the first time I heard Classical Music.

First Impression of Classical Music

> *I was sitting at the kitchen table eating soup, I think. Any who, my grandfather had his old radio on 88.1 FM. He liked to listen to sports on the radio. I don't know who was playing, but I heard violins softly whispering notes. While the cello danced with the bass in sweet harmony and I thought, "My goodness. I want to play music like that!" I asked my grandfather what type of music was playing on the radio. He said Classical. Then granddaddy let it play for another minute before he asked me to change the station to his baseball game. I've been a fan of Classical Music ever since. I don't know all the ins and outs of Classical music. I just know it speaks to my soul, like no other music does. For that I am grateful. (Flashback Over)*

Here I was at fifteen years old, with millions of other teenagers, ready to talk to congressmen and women about the "teen pregnancy" epidemic in America. Well I met former Congresswoman Nancy Johnson and Congressman Chris Dodd of Connecticut. I spoke to them about some of my friends, whose parents kicked them out of the house, because they were pregnant. I told them I was fortunate that my Grams took me in and helped me. The whole family helped me graduate high school and raised my daughter. It takes a village to raise a child. Especially, when you are still a child yourself.

Well, to our astonishment Congress passed the Children's Act of 1988. It was to give teen-parents the authority of an adult to raise their children. It had other things in there that WE, teen advocates, didn't know. Just like policy today. You go in thinking you are getting what will help communities and someone changes or adds language that under cuts the original intent. This is probably a good place to talk about my first testimony at Connecticut's Legislative Office Building.

2 Connecticut Judiciary Committee Room

My First Testimony at Connecticut's State Capitol

"I hope I don't make an ass out of myself." It was the night before I testified before the Judiciary Committee. My thoughts were racing about what I should say or should not say. I have my notes and my testimony was already submitted. I need to look professional. Let's see what's in the closet. "Damn! It's 3:00am. I have to get up in four hours!" I looked at a pants suit that was one of my favorites. I ironed it and hung it up on the bedroom door. I sat on the bed and took a deep breath. "Buttons, you did this when you were fifteen. They are people too. Don't get to hot headed if someone says something insulting. Remember what you learned in Public Speaking class. If you get stuck, take a drink of water, then proceed." My self-talk helped. Then I laid down thanking God for the opportunity to give back again.

I woke up that morning with little sleep. I felt like a kid on Christmas! I had printed a copy of my testimony. I was off to the State Capitol in Hartford, CT. It was a very long day. "As a voting taxpayer of Connecticut, who took the day off from work, I should be heard first," I thought to myself. I look around the room at all the "regular folk" who took time off to testify. I felt angry all of a sudden. "Why do we have to wait? Why is PAID staff going first eating up the time?" These were the questions I asked Mr. Lopez while I was waiting to speak. His prompt response was, "You should have been here a year ago. It was worse. We literally had to take a stand in this very room to have them start alternating between state officials and the public." I silently sighed and felt dis-empowered. Then I thought, I would mention it before I speak. Hours went by and then it was my turn. I talked about how a Certificate of Rehabilitation or a Provisional Pardon would only be wasted paper, no different than the stack of awards, certificates, and degrees I have at home. I still cannot get a decent job, if I left my current one nor any housing, because of the discrimination I face having a felony. When I finished speaking, former Representative Green asked me some thoughtful questions. I only remember one, "What can we do, my colleagues and I to help someone like you?" I simply said, "Give me a REAL SECOND CHANCE."

This was the beginning of my road back to advocacy! I started as A Board member for a non-profit. At the time I didn't know my testimony was against the bill my organization was pushing to pass. After a year of traveling and reading about criminal justice and drug policy. I wanted to organize and train leaders on these issues. When a position became available. I resigned as a board member to apply for the Lead Organizer position and got it! It was a tough interview facing five people, including a philanthropist. I started my first and only Community Organizer job on April 16, 2007. Within a year I was promoted to Policy Director and finally, the Director of Strategic Relations for this Connecticut non-profit. I worked on everything from street lights, closing prisons, to international drug policy reform before I was done. I will never forget my first leadership team, Clean Slate Committee, CSC.

Working with CSC

My first group was the CSC. Our first order of business was to advocate for removing the parole ban, former Governor Rell, put on Connecticut. This is what happened: two parolees met at a halfway house and started conspiring about how they were going to burglarize a home in Cheshire, CT. It went south fast. What they did to the females in that family is unthinkable. What the husband/father had suffered through I wish on no man. No, I will not give you the details of that horrific encounter, if you choose you can Google it. The result was a ban on parole for the state of Connecticut. Which meant, no one could get paroled and everyone on parole was sent back to jail. The CSC and I began discussing how this "Ban" was affecting our community and people we know and love. This resulted in my first community meeting in Hartford, Connecticut.

My First Community Meeting as Lead Community Organizer

The CSC was a group of community individuals, who represented unheard voices in different political or "power" rooms. We had people who were formally incarcerated, youth, elderly, Whites, Blacks, Browns, family members of formally/currently incarcerated people, educators, suburban, urban and rural males and females, business men/women and sometimes the neighborhood Black police officer's. Clean Slate Committee, so named after the very piece of legislation I spoke out against at my first hearing, began doing research on the parole ban. For weeks we were getting complaints and decided former Governor Rell had to answer to our wounded community.

After doing a power analysis and connecting with seasoned community organizers, CSC began letting everyone know, "We invited Gov. Rell to a Community Meeting and she said, Yes!" We were on a high as a group and me as an Organizer! We had our logistics down; the order of questions; who was chairing; video/camera setups; press release...EVERYTHING was set and ready to go!

The night of the meeting it was a packed house. My boss at the time said, "If it's a success it belongs to the leaders. If it's a failure it belongs to the Organizer and that my dear is, YOU." My heart dropped, because all I wanted to do was make him proud! More than that I really believed I had finally belonged to a group that understood me without question. I wanted the team to be proud of me. After that comment, I politely excused myself and went to make sure everyone remembered their positions and we had enough food, Lol!

I tell you ignorance is bliss! I was sure the governor was going to show up! She didn't! What she did do was send the Commissioner of Corrections, the Chair of Pardons & Parole, the Chair of Public Safety and two extra staff members. They were in the hot seat and they knew it, lol! The Commissioner of Corrections, Teresa Lantz, handled herself fairly well. She lost her cool a few times though. Lantz made the typical "Powers that be," mistake...underestimating educated youth and Average Joes on the issue. In the end Clean Slate Committee got all those officials to agree to meet twice a month at a community center in Hartford, CT. The Ban was eventually lifted, and the group was seen as a powerhouse of change.

The CSC and I would successfully override former Governor Rell's veto for our 'Ban The Box' legislative campaign to provide equal job opportunity for people with criminal history. That story I will save for another book. Let's just say, this national campaign made it all the way to the White House! Former, President Barack Obama signed an Executive Order, "Banning The Box" on Federal employment opportunities. Even the EEOC (Equal Employment Opportunity Commission), have regulations and guidelines. Our campaign became a model to follow. We started at the local municipal level and while advocating on the state level, we were participating in national efforts for change. This began my national recognition in the drug policy and criminal justice reform movement. This recognition lead to me moving to California in 2015 to work for a fellow advocate and community leader in the struggle. It was in California were my psychosomatic seizures began and the discovery of my true self began. This did not happen in the most pleasant of circumstances. It happened the way a Lotus Flower blooms. In the most horrendous conditions!

Remember, this is not your traditional book. It is how my mind now functions. Trying to figure out connections in my life as to why now I have PTSD. One story triggers another. Some are good memories. Others are life lessons. This is a life lesson that made me choice to be single until…

Getting Answers: Warren

As I am writing this book I will share what happens in a day that is not part of my journal section. For example, today, Sunday, July 3, 2016. I don't think I will ever let myself forget, how Self-Victimization can be cruel and kind. I will not soon forget the day Warren dismissed me. I have been cast aside many times, sad to say. I have done my own dismissing of individuals. I have never in all my years been dumped in such a nice way…with a hug.

Before I even get into it, let me say this…If you EVER want me to PERMANETLY LEAVE YOU ALONE…just say I'm not a child of Yahweh/God! I mean, call me demonic or accuse me of putting a hex on you and I am done with you for good! It is a sure-fire way of me letting you go without remorse or guilt. No need to apologize or reconnect. It lets me know something about you, more than hurting my feelings. What's that? If you have to ask then you need to think a little deeper than the surface, lol.

Remember it was June 17th, 2016, when Warren ejected me out of his home. That was two weeks ago! Well after last week's battle to not kill myself, by taking a substantial number of pills. I was eager to get my Pyrite stone from Warren. I thought this was going to end different. However, I did expect more from Warren. He had avoided me and MOST of my text messages since he dismissed me from his home. Since, every attempt I made prior to going over his house to collect my few belongings were rejected. I made the transfer of my Pyrite easy. I simply told Warren to put my stuff in a bag and place it on the bench outside his front door. Warren agreed and then injected that I could knock and say Hi. I took this as a choice not an obligation.

When you have PTSD or any mental disorder it is hard to stay positive or optimistic. I remember a time when all my thoughts were optimistic. Today I struggle to keep hope alive. Even knowing that positive thinking brings positive results. I hope the Universe doesn't punish me because my emotions are not matching up with what I know to be true. EVERYTHING WILL WORK OUT FOR MY GOOD!

Back to meeting up with Warren! I showered got dressed and encouraged myself that this was going to be easy. "Just drive there, park and get the bag! Easy Peasy! No need to talk or see him." All the self-talk in the world could not prepare me for this crazy ass conversation.

When I got to Warren's house my bag was not outside on the bench. I had to knock. If I knew knocking would lead to me being accused of NOT being supportive and putting a hex on him. I would have asked him to leave it on Candy's porch. Yes, I am extremely vexed! I was so hurt by him. He was oblivious to my pain or that I might even be hurt. I got to stop picking men! I swear I got to stop! Here is how the situation went down:

Warren: Hey, how you doing?

Me: I am fine. Just came for my stuff. *(Look at the chair NEAR the front door and grabbed my stuff.)* Thanks. I will see you later.

Warren: You have time to talk for a minute?

Me: Sure. *(We walk to the back porch. His dogs missed me so much, they just jumped and kissed my face and hands.)*

Warren: I have so much I want to say, I just don't trust myself to say it right.

Me: Just say it. We are adults. Just be honest.

Warren: Well, I told you I didn't want to be in a relationship. I felt like you were pushing me into something. Remember I told you about the girl who was wearing my clothes. She thought we were in a relationship?

Me: I wasn't looking for a relationship. Nor did I believe you and I were having one. I thought we were just enjoying our friendship and being with someone who understood our spirituality.

Warren: Well, a few things happened that made me feel like I should back off. When Babs pulled away from you that day and avoided you I took that as a sign. Then my Mom sent me that horrible text. Also, I should have stayed at my school reunion, because it was the last time I would have to speak with the people I needed to see.

Me: *(Shocked and applaud look on my face. I stopped petting Babs, who stayed next to me the whole time wanting me to pet her.)* Hold on. First, you can see there isn't a problem with me and the dogs. Secondly, you are going to have to accept your mother is jealous of ANY woman in your life. Thirdly, I could have stayed home alone. I am a big girl and would have been fine.

Warren: I thought you needed my support. So, I stayed.

Me: NO! I told you to go back. *Silence.* Listen, I learned something new about myself. Literally, in the last day. I missed my dad so much that I would allow others to cause me harm. Just so I could belong to a Man. I want to tell you that the day I made you so anxious and left. You really hurt me. I felt rejected and abandon.

Warren: *Pushes his seat back in shock.* I felt rejected and abandon! I asked you to keep me company and you went and took a nap.

Me: I can see how you would feel that way. However, you told me that you did not want my help. You wanted to accomplish fixing up your house yourself. Secondly, I told you I felt sick and needed to lay down.

Warren: I did say I didn't want help. I did want to have conversation with you. I needed your help to get up and down the ladder. There is more to it than that. Having company means you are with that person in the same room.

Me: Yes, however, I was sick and needed to lay down. I took the dogs with me so you wouldn't be disturbed. You could have asked me to help, instead of asking me to leave. *Silence.*

Warren: I'm glad we are talking. See this clears up somethings. It is a beginning. The other thing is I told you I never been with a person so into their spirituality. I been with women who feel the total opposite of my spiritual belief. You are so into your spirituality. Like now I can feel what other people are feeling. I was always empathetic. Now it's like way too much. I can't go into the bathroom and calm down anymore.

Me: Well Welcome to my world! Ever since June 8, 2015 I pick up a great deal of different energies and emotions from people. It causes me to have my tremors. The exercises we did opened your Chakras and your third-eye. I thought that is what you wanted.

Warren: Yeah, well, *(chuckling.)* Like remember the stealth helicopter and the light. There is a helicopter that comes through here all the time. The light we saw is because there is a train. So, you...

Me: *Interrupting*, Hold on I did see a stealth helicopter! You pointed it out to me. I'm glad to know there is a train. *(Thinking to myself...What the fuck he is getting at. I KNOW I don't hallucinate or have delusions.)*

Warren: Well, you are spiritually strong, and I thought you put a Santeria spell or something on me *(half laughing, half serious.)* Like my Mom with the text, the dog not wanting to come to you and me feeling to open to the world.

Me: *Sternly.* Yes, I know Santeria a little! I know Buddhism a little! The anklet I wear is from my Santeria Godfather for protection against evil and negativity. It ages you to do evil. It cost you your life. I don't do that shit! I just know enough to light candles for my protection and do petitions for Love, Health and Prosperity. If you knew how much money I spent trying to cleanse myself of negativity, generational curses! I spent $1800 to $2000. I went to Sweat Logs, Crystal Healing, I had my soul cleanse from contracts. All kinds of shit! Because I thought I was tainted... *I begin to choke back my tears. He doesn't deserve to see me cry! He doesn't deserve to see the pain he just caused me with that bullshit!* I got to leave. Good-bye Warren.

In a matter of five steps I was at the front door. Warren stopped me. Then asked me for a hug. I hesitated. Then God said, pray and let it go. So I hugged him and told him to trust himself more. That was the end of Warren and me. It also was the beginning of me isolating myself, once again afraid of the world and it's hurtful people. Being super sensitive to other people's energies is difficult when you don't know how to utilize it properly. I know I've been given a gift. I just need a teacher to guide me through my new gift's purpose.

I take responsibility for my part in the situation with Warren. I should have never trusted another man, so quickly after being mentally, emotionally and physically abused. I did!

Because of that whole thing with Warren, I even abused myself. I called my ex-husband and had sex with him. It was fabulous! However, not what I truly needed. It was a coping mechanism. I just wanted to be desired even if it wasn't healthy for me. That's the illness of being a sexually abused child, teen, and adult. You keep doing it to yourself until YOU HAD ENOUGH! Perhaps even after that, because it is so familiar. I cannot tell you how often I used sex for instant gratification. Only to later regret that decision. I even thought about asking my ex-husband if I can be his live-in house keeper! How sick and twisted is that?! Just so I can feel safe.

41

I am learning daily to end old harmful habits. It's not easy breaking away from what is familiar. If it were just a change of mind or knowing the root cause to make you stop, then anyone with a vice would no longer have or feel the need to return to it.

On Sunday, July 17, 2016, I texted Warren and told him. He was not the VICTIM in our situation. I was. I mean really! If I could cast some spell to get a man, don't you think I would choose someone with more to offer me than companionship? I am motivated by intellect not bank accounts! Furthermore, I damn sure don't want a MOMMA'S BOY, who's every decision is based on her purse strings! Come on give me a break! I have more value than what you have in your bank account. I have more value than anyone can imagine or think. I offer a person something that is rare. When it is gone, you feel it in your soul. It is my love. **My love is PRICELESS!**

Thoughts of Love

by LaResse Harvey - 1/5/2007

What is Pure Love?

If I did not choose to love you, yet love happens. Is that Pure?

Did Love choose me to love you?

Did Love choose you to love me?

What happens when you come across individuals who don't know how to love? What can we teach them?

What is Pure Love?

Is Pure Love loving someone because they exist?

Isn't that how God Loves Us?

Or is it about a Man who loves a Broken Woman,

Like Hosea loved his wife in the Old Testament?

Perhaps Pure Love is...

Discovering how to love yourself.

You taking the time to Love YOU is the purest form of Love.

That's when you learn how to love healthy enough to give it in return.

The Journey Continues

I am glad you continue to take time to read about my journey. Most people are not this complex. Maybe I am underestimating the average person, lol. In any event, this is the part of my life when I tell you how I lost everything to gain my soul! What have you lost because of past traumas or vices? Do you even recognize how you compromised your own values and ethics to stay with someone or stay on a job? We can all rationalize our way out of the choices we made. We can all find excuses. What we need is understanding and to be understanding.

I was so willing to sacrifice my own needs to help others. My motive was to belong. I just wanted to be loved. I think I was too nice. Maybe it was the company I kept that made me feel like being helpful was a bad thing. I gave until I had nothing left except the will to survive. I didn't have hope. I was in the dark. I was existing without purpose or plan. I didn't have anything figured out or knew what I was going to do next. I trusted people with my finances and my life. I lost confidence in myself and my ability to decide. I don't know if you know what that feels like. I don't have anything to compare it to. What I do know is living life without hope is not living at all. Being helpful to people you love isn't wrong. I was loving the wrong people and forgot to love myself in the process. I thought when I get to California I would be free. Unfortunately, it was were my illness began. Now let's continue with Button's Journey.

California Is A Bust!

This is an overview of a happy adventure that went south in a matter of a year! I've told myself on several occasions, that I wasn't in my right frame of mind. I was dealing with my PTSD and many decisions I made were irrational. Some people did down right shady shit! None of this was helping me heal. It only added to my depression. When I accept that during that time I was learning to let go, I can find a place to begin healing. I can look back at it with a gentleness towards myself and see how I was a victim of myself. There were people who played their roles, don't get me wrong. However, I was a willing participant at times. Other times I just wasn't mentally there. You will learn how I met Phi, Q, Dragon, Jade and Misty. You will read about my darkest time and how I found my way back to Connecticut. As you travel through my emotional roller-coaster with me, please don't forget that I have severe depression, chronic post traumatic disorder and severe anxiety. Which means, you have been reading how my mind is dysfunctional. It contradicts itself because of my emotions. I have ups and downs. I jump all over the place, because I cannot really focus to long on one story or I will get stuck. Thank you for being here and continuing to read my story. Even though it isn't the "traditional" way of telling a story, lol.

***Note: If any part of this causes you to reflect on your own choices, please don't feel stuck there. Reflect, write it down and share it with someone you love or burn it. You can even share it with me. If you need to stop reading parts of this section, because it's too painful, please do. Skip to the end if you feel the need. Don't force yourself into a space you aren't emotionally prepared for. Give yourself time. I totally understand. Some stories hit too close to home. If you or someone you know is in an abusive situation, please get help and find a safe way to do it.

Life in California

During my stay in California I became ill with psychosomatic seizures and chronic PTSD. It happened weeks after my 43rd birthday. I had an easy job. I was helping women reenter back into society from incarceration. I went to work happy. I had my own office and I loved listening to the needs of the woman. I even helped other staff. It was there I met Misty. We hit it off great. We were both nerds. I started going out with Misty after work to karaoke. It was at karaoke when I first met Dragon, Phi and Q. Thursday nights at Denny's was live, lol! I found friends and we all loved the same things.

When I was home, I would spend time with my next-door neighbor's daughter. She was 19 and finishing up cosmetology school. Because I had my license, she and I would talk about her classes and homework. I even let her practice make-up on me, lol. It was fun! After a few months I met Jade and KT. Jade was the friend of my neighbor's daughter. KT was my neighbor's cousin. They all called me Ma.

I don't know exactly when my life became unmanageable. I just knew that when I started making decisions based on my emotions and not the facts. I got lost in wanting to belong. I got lost in being in California. I didn't notice I was losing ground until the ground was no longer there. Let's start where it began to go downhill...my birthday.

Celebrating My 43rd Birthday!

I woke up with excitement and fear. This was going to be the first time in twenty-two years that I would have a party in my home. Twenty-two years since that fatal night on May 22, 1993. The night I got jumped by two associates. Until now, I hadn't trusted anyone enough to have a Birthday Party at my home. "Well, I am in a new state and no one knows me. This is a way for a few colleagues and neighbors to get to know me." I felt great in-spite of the constant invasive thoughts about stabbing and killing someone. "I hope everyone I invited shows up. There will be about seven to ten people. That's plenty of people to have fun and small enough to keep me safe," I told myself.

I took a shower and went to work. I called Dragon to make sure he was able to help me setup for the party. "Dragon I will be at your house at 5:15pm. Please be ready. I am nervous, so if I talk a great deal today just go with it." I hung up the phone. I thought about going to the dispensary first prior to picking Dragon up. I am so excited about living in a state that approves medicinal cannabis for PTSD. I was shocked when the doctor diagnosed me with having Combat PTSD, because I wasn't a soldier. I recall him telling me that because of being in jail for almost six years and having to continuously defend myself that my anxiety was like someone who'd been at war. I agreed, because he didn't know the half of it.

It was about 5:25pm when I picked Dragon up. I left work at 5:04pm. Now that I think about it, I don't remember what I did at work that day. I know I received a few cards with money, so I can buy furniture. I did a 'GoFundMe' page and a few people donated. I bought a kitchen table set and fake leather futon. But work that day escapes me. I drove up to Dragon's house and he gets in. "Here eat this with me." Dragon looked at the Rice Krispy treat with an odd glance. "It's an edible! If you are going to help me I need you calm, so you don't freak out. I'm the only person who can freak out today!" Dragon took the tiniest bite. "Okay. Now what do you need me to cook?" I told him I purchased chicken wings and a veggie tray but if we needed anything else "let's get it now". Dragon is a great chef. He is good at explaining what he is doing too. I personally think he should have is own 'Cooking and All Things MacGyver' show.

The food was set. The decorations were set. Now let's start the party! During the evening we ate, played puzzle games, had drinks and me...I smoked my cannabis! It's nice to see how people can come together and have fun no strings attached. Even one of my friends from Connecticut came to celebrate with me! I asked Dragon why he wasn't with Misty. It was clear to me that both were attracted to and deeply cared for one another. Dragon explained that Misty just got out of a long-term relationship and didn't want to be tied down. He would love to be in a relationship with her, but he didn't really have anything to offer her as a man. Dragon had open heart surgery about three years ago. He hadn't been able to work and could only stand or do an activity in short spurts. He was on County Assistance and couldn't fully contribute financially. "I'm sure Misty isn't so shallow that she wouldn't date you. Women want a man to have more than a huge bank account these days." I said. Dragon shrugged but thought it might be a great idea to at least talk to Misty about it again at a later date. The party ended at 3am the next day! I never had so much fun doing "Geek and Nerd" things, lol.

Becoming Mentally Ill

After my birthday party was a hit, Misty, Dragon and I became pretty close. Days turned into weeks and before you knew it, June had arrived, and I got sick. It happened on June 8, 2015, when I had my first psychosomatic-seizures. On one hand it was a spiritual experience. On the other it is a living nightmare.

(Flashback) I mean since I was fourteen I've been paying my way to live. Even while incarcerated, I had two jobs to ease the burden of my family having to send sending me money. What I don't understand is why in the Hell does it take so damn long to receive support when you need it? I am very upset about this ordeal with Social Security Disability. (Flashback Over) Let me get off my tangent. You want to know more about California, right?

Misty, Dragon and I hung out every day. I had another psychosomatic-seizure on July 17th, 2015 and stayed in the hospital for two days. I asked Dragon to move in with me. Oh boy! I jumped ahead of myself.

Okay during the month of May and June I was dating Misty's best friend, Smokey. He was a quiet guy, who did security at a bar. On our first date, I fell for him hard. I believe my heart was ready to love freely without question. FYI that was a huge mistake to give of oneself without even knowing the person.

As the weeks went by, Misty's best friend and I went on several dates. For my birthday we all went to Universal Studios. I felt like a big kid, lol! It was exciting, and I had no problem showing my affection towards Smokey. He was like a big teddy bear. He knew how to make me smile, lol. Any who, Smokey was still deeply in-love with his ex-girlfriend, which I found out the hard way.

I decided in July that I waited long enough for him after he stood me up one too many times. In my world if I am giving you everything, then it should be reciprocated. Well, between the first seizure and the second seizure incident. I was Facebook Messenging with Q.

When I was in the hospital, Q came to visit. Smokey never showed up. Even my friend Maisie came to visit. She left me a note, so I would know she came to visit. But Q was the only one who stayed until I woke up and spoke with the doctors. He was my little advocate. Q even got in the hospital bed with me, lol. It was a special moment. Of course, he romanced me, and I fell for him. Smokey and I had been on break. I thought Q was the "perfect" man for me. Then Q showed his true colors.

The Break UP with Q!

"Baby look at my check! I got $75 dollars more for take home!" Q was excited about his paycheck. He was jumping and dancing around. "I know. I told you that would happen. That's why I changed the W2 for you," I said. I wasn't as excited as him. I figure as an adult you shouldn't act like a kid when getting more take home pay. Especially, when the money is already spent on the light bill. "Can't you be a bit more excited?" Q was irritated, and his voice and posture became aggressive. "Listen, I cannot get excited over $75. That's how much the light bill is this month, because we used the AC. I will be excited when it is $75 in OUR pockets, not a bill." I stated firmly, "Please calm down and let me take my medicine." Q went into the shower. While he was in the shower, I rolled a blunt and smoked. We talked about his behavior and my response the next morning.

On Sunday morning after Q was dressed for church, he walked up on me while I was sitting on the bed. As Q hunched over me in a threatening stance, I looked up and asked him to back up. I started to roll a blunt. "Q please don't stand over me like that," I stated in a matter-of-fact tone. Q stepped closer and pushed his shoulders forward as if he was calling me out to a fight. I responded again, "Just let me smoke and we can talk about your extra cash. I am not impressed. I'm the one that told you, you would get extra money in your check. Now PLEASE, step back. If you don't move back, I'm not responsible." Q stepped closer with balled fist and pushed his shoulders forward again and said, "What you going to do if I don't?" Before I can think, I had him by the throat with my left hand and was punching him in the stomach and ribs. He was a few inches off the ground!

Let me give you a visual. Q weighs about 280 pounds and is 5 feet 7 inches. I am 175 pounds and 5 feet 7 inches. It looked like Mush Mouth lifting Fat Albert, lol! Well let's just say if it wasn't for Dragon, Jade and Phi, I might be behind bars again. That's why I packed his stuff and told him to go. When Q returned from church with his best friend, the crew handled it. I stayed away. Never thought I would have another rage blackout again. But I did. After that I tried not to get too upset. It didn't last long. I still get angry, I just didn't blackout. Thanks to coping techniques. However, my psychosomatic-seizures have gotten worse.

After I broke up with Q, Phi was eagerly waiting to jump in to take Q's place. I didn't see the signs because I was doped up on Zoloft! I thought I found a true friend and lover in Phi. Little did I know he was only sticking around for the money! To relive those moments with Phi is very painful and still raw to this day. I will try and give you a glimpse of this relationship that was doomed from the beginning. Jade tried to warn me, but I didn't listen. I didn't want to believe her because I needed Phi's help! At first, I stayed to protect his daughter from him. Soon the shock of being evicted took a toll on me. No social security. No unemployment disability. No money. No home. No hope!

Phi was the only person that helped me moved most of my stuff from the apartment. I secured storage at his aunt's house. Then he asked me to move in with him and his daughter. Phi was renting a room in Long Beach, CA. It was a four-bedroom house. It was here, living with rodents in the walls and roaches everywhere that I became dark and bleak.

My Breakdown Moment

On December 11, 2016 I had a nervous breakdown. I went into my prayer closet and smashed all the glasses of water and saints I had on it. I lost my faith, and everything went black. I had cut my wrist and fingers. The stress of being evicted and everyday Phi warning about California's eviction laws was too much. I was angry at God/Yahweh and myself. Maybe if I knew my rights, I could've fought a little. I could have salvaged my apartment. I didn't. I couldn't. For two months I lived in rat and roach invested places. I stayed in hotels and I helped Phi get a place in Nevada, a place he wanted to live.

I am going to let you into my state of mind from that moment when I went into my prayer closet and smashed my alter to pieces. I just knew God had forsaken me for all my wrongs. Blood was everywhere. I had to wait for Jade to come home before I went to the hospital. I wrapped my wrist in a towel to stop the bleeding. I was now headed in the direction of Hell on Earth. I felt lost, confused, and empty. I was a hallow shell.

It was then I began to write in journals to keep track of my days and emotional outbursts. I wanted to record whether I was or wasn't getting better mentally. I realized since December 30, 2015 I have been homeless. I have lived with people out of desperation. I would have made different decisions, if I was healthy in mind, body, and spirit. I am still battling with positive and negative thoughts. It is in the next chapter I will show you how my mind functions with PTSD. I will call these pages, *The Journals*. You will read about a mind lost in emotional anguish without hope for a better anything. A confused adult lost in a childlike cognitive state. Just like a child desperate for love, forgiveness and acceptance. I wondered what it would be like to have someone to love me.

Obviously, Phi wasn't all bad. It only takes 90 days to see the truth behind the person. In the beginning Phi seemed matured. I ignored his earlier emotional outburst. I forgot about conversations he had about his sexuality. I trusted Phi enough to think for me, because he was there. He helped me store the things I needed at his mother's house. Phi let me live with him and his daughter. He was patient with me in the beginning. Most days I didn't do anything. I forced myself to take showers. I engaged in mild conversation. Then Phi started having outbursts and blaming me for shit I didn't understand. Once you read these two Journal entries you'll get a better idea. I trusted Phi to take care of me. Whenever he told me to do something. I did it. I was lifeless. He helped me distract myself from negative thoughts, by showing me Summoner's War. It is a monster video game. Well Summoner's War is more than that. I still play it! It helps me relax.

Phi tried to normalize our days. In the morning we would get up and get his daughter ready for school. After doing the normal brush your teeth and wash your face routine. We head out the door and walk two blocks to the school. Phi knew I was sad. He tried to make me laugh. One day he purposefully tripped himself. I laughed the whole day. Then my sadness grew deeper. Phi felt he wasn't doing enough. Things changed when he returned his daughter to her mother. It was like, the frustration he would have for his daughter, Phi began to take out on me.

Phi would punish his daughter by keeping her the corner for an hour. At first, he would beat her and yell. Then I suggested making her stand in the corner. Tell her what she did wrong. I was so depressed I never knew she was there for that long. Between the medications, smoking marijuana and my mental state. I was in a fog. A very numb fog. I didn't feel anything anymore. I didn't care if I lived or died. I was the walking dead on the inside.

Because of Phi keeping his daughter in the corner for so long. The state came to investigate. The police were called for child abuse. One of Phi's house mates reported him. I freaked out and was relieved at the same time. Because I knew the baby was safe. We had dropped her back off to her Mom's house the day before the police showed up. Now I just have to worry about me. It really didn't matter anymore. I was too far in.

To give you a glimpse of what it was like. I have included some moments from my journal that highlight my thoughts and behaviors. This includes Phi's behaviors as well.

Moments of Chaos Recorded

January 15, 2016

I'm trying to cope with the fact many people want to hear from me. I don't want to talk to anyone! I barely want to talk to my daughter. My former self is gone. I'm developing a different me. The hard part is figuring out exactly who that is again. I knew who I was. I knew my purpose and mission. Now, I'm back to square one. There are fragments of my former self I see rise now and then. A mere shell of what was a powerful strong Black woman. Now I feel like a feeble old lady. Like I'm waiting for God to play the cruelest trick of all...DEATH. Would that be the best ending for me now or later? I grow tired of trying to be patient about HOPE FAITH God's promise. Is there even a God? Or do we WILL Him so there is someone/thing to blame for our own calamities? What if it is about Will and Will alone? We will God to be real, so we never have to face our personal failures as human beings. What rhyme or reason is there for a father to sexually assault his first, second only daughter? I guess men will say, "Child" because they got molested and rape too. I'm not a man. I am a woman and as much as my dad wanted/willed a boy I am a GIRL!

For so long I tried to figure out why shit happened to me. I felt cursed. A target for hurt, pain, suffering and anguish. I tried for 43 years to be optimistic about life. Take my punches, throw a few good licks back. Learn about strategic, critical and analytical thinking. Positive thought, hypnosis spiritual and religious beliefs from all over the world. Only to still end up empty and lost. "ABBA! ABBA! ABBA! Father why have thou forsaken me?" Jesus said. I thought about some things. IF God loves His children and we are to do greater things than Christ...Why haven't we? Oh, yeah, here is the caveat – Be IN this World, but not OF it! How the fuck you supposed to be IN something and NOT OF IT?!!! Are WE like PUSSY?!

I'm truly happy about so many other things, I feel like I'm split in two worlds. I don't want to go back and yet I can't go too far ahead because I'm stuck. Somewhere in me is a stuck child looking, screaming, yelling for her father and He, God, may not even want her/me! I keep shaking because I feel like God has forsaken me. No matter how many times I try to look at the positive. I keep feeling sad. I'm trying not to hurt Phi. It's not working. When I try to explain what is happening, he thinks it's related to him. Even though it is <u>NOT</u>! I don't know what people want from me! I'm doing the best I can to get healthy. I don't know if I will ever be the same again. I don't get it?! Why do I have to STOP in the middle of my PTSD trigger/breakdown...whatever and consider someone else. Isn't that how I got here? Considering everyone else but me?!! All because of a sentence about me being like everyone else. I hate when people say that! What Phi can't decipher is generalization comments from direct or indirect ones!

It's getting harder to decipher even harder not to get mad at myself for it. I'm so messed up. My mind knows better but my emotions are tears, sadness, anger and fear. Why am I afraid? Why am I hurting? It's not matching up. People think it's easy to stop. It is not. I count myself a champion for self-development and self-determination. Now I feel lost. Like what I know or "think" I know isn't REAL or RIGHT! I just don't understand it. All my schooling, working, reading, MY FAITH!!!!! ALL IN QUESTION!!! Who am I now? I don't want to turn evil, mean or cruel, because of this situation. I just want to enjoy my life without feeling like I'm just here until you don't need or want me anymore. It's crazy because I know that's not true in my current relationship or situation. It's not the best but it is okay. I'm happy most of the time. Then these thoughts happen like a runaway train. It can start from a feeling of being attacked and go to being alone and feeling worthless. Why can't I just bounce back like before? Just let the shit go instantly? Sometimes I can. The times I can't it gets like this!

Phi's response to me, "You taught me a very valuable lesson. People been telling me this for years. You can't keep or make someone happy, who isn't happy with themselves. I feel like there is no reason to try anymore. I'm supposed to look at everything on the bright side. When I thought like that people told me I was wrong for thinking this way. Everything is so fucking bad for everyone else. But my own daughter doesn't love me. She loves someone else as her MOM. No one does shit for me for free! I can't even borrow a $1 from my family without paying it back. If you don't have to be happy I don't have to be happy. You feel like you've been forsaken. You think you the only person who's been fondled. How do you think I feel? I was fondled. I was forced to fondle others. How do you think I feel about that?"

I have stopped crying and started writing down everything Phi continues to say. "I wish witchcraft, demons and super powers were real, so I can hurt everyone who's hurting me, causing me to feel badly. Mothafuckas think I am happy. Like their life is so bad. I'm supposed to look for happiness, why? When Mothafuckas around you aren't happy. I can do what I want and not give a fuck about their happiness. Doing what the fuck I want makes me happy. That's why I want to travel, see the world and do what the fuck I want. No one cares, loves, or respects me like I do them! This is stupid. We just wasting each other's time. God gave me what I wanted. I wanted my daughter. She loves someone else more than me. Then on top of that, she's a bad ass little girl. She does what she wants and doesn't care how I feel or how it makes me feel! I got a good woman and she's not happy with herself. Fuck this PTSD shit! Fuck everyone! Even though I want to say fuck God. I can't! Because I believe in my heart that God is real. I know he is in my heart. It's not something to blame shit on. I believe Jesus died for all my sins. I don't give a fuck about the Illuminati, if that's real or who made the shit up!"

Phi would continue his rant and my ability to process my own thoughts were short circuited because he had to be worse off than me. I just need some peace and quiet. Why does everything have to be a competition with him? One day I will make a list of things I dislike about him and see if HE measures up to my standards. Right now, he is all I have in this mess. I am homeless. I live in a small room with him and his daughter, in a house with rats in the walls and roaches everywhere. What did I do to deserve this? Boy, what would my children and family think of me now, if they saw me? I can't let anyone know I have fallen so far from where I started. I should've never moved to California! This is some bullshit! I'm just going to shut down.

March 5, 2016

I'm getting tired of being the "BAD GUY" when it comes to Phi. How about his fucked-up behaviors? Let me list them one by one!

1. Extreme Jealousy!

2. Inability to take information that is factual to negate negative emotions.

3. Okay for him to constantly talk and say negative, derogatory things about himself and me! Yet I can't wake up not liking myself.

4. Only cares about how 'HE' thinks feels, believes, and desires things to be! If I behave in this manner he packs his clothes and says I'm making it ALL about me. **BULLSHIT!!!**

5. No matter who I am talking to or discussing my life with, he immediately thinks I'm going to leave him!

6. If I get up to PEE or go to the window in a T-shirt. I am accused of cheating! Or flaunting my body and/ or being DISRESPECTFUL to him. When I go to the window in my t-shirt it is a little above my knee. The same length as these little tight dresses he wants me to wear. He admits because of his PAST relationships he is nervous. Yet he is NOT working on his Jealousy, but he wants me to work on my anger. HYPROCRATE!!!

7. IF I try to discuss something about THE RELATIONSHIIP. He **ASSUMES** *I'm talking* **BAD** *about him OR I* **don't WANT** *him. DUMB ASS! When I talk about what's wrong in a calm voice without being defensive, so HE can HEAR AND CHANGE what was happening, he blows up and gets me all perturbed then blames me!*

8. *Every time he gets mad he immediately goes to "No one loves me. No one respects me or cares what my feelings are." Bullshit! It's like why am I here? I wonder what it means to him that I stay here taking his* **BULLSHIT TOO***!! He is not the* <u>ONLY ONE</u> *dealing with a Broken Person!*

9. *Sex does not resolve anything, PHI! Nor is it great when you don't know how to warm the woman up after you denigrate her character 5 times a day!*

10. *Whenever I want to talk about one of my "Real" past relationships. He interrupts with his story of similarity or worse. This is NOT a competition! Never does he pick up on the fact that HE doesn't show me the love I want. He shows me the love he can give, and I have to accept that! He hasn't matured enough to realize the love you have in your head is fantasy. You have to look for ways the person shows love.* **NOT HOW YOU WANT TO BE LOVED!** *That was a hard lesson for me to grasp. It was that way of thinking that helped to destroy all my relationships. Looking for how I want to be loved, instead at looking at how that person shows love. I would whine they didn't love me because I felt disrespected by different things they did. Well, the only person who thought they were disrespectful was me. When I talked to other women they laughed at me and said, "I was crazy!" I understand that shit now. Boy! Do I get it! If you have someone there who makes sure your basics are being met; you are a good sex partner; plus, you want to spend time doing mostly the same things. Than hunker down and relax for the rest of your life! The other shit you look for isn't necessary when you reach 40. You realize you wasted time arguing about some dumb shit like unrealistic Respect! Too old to dispute or argue about shit I can't control. Just like no one can control my thoughts and feelings. I can't control anyone's emotions or thoughts. However, when given accurate information up against my emotions and what I THINK is happening. I must succumb to the facts and tell my emotions they are NOT REAL, just residual effects.*

No photos during this time.

I didn't want to exist.

Therefore, I did not…to

myself.

11. *Phi needs to desperately deal with feelings of abandonment. I can't help. If I could I would heal my own first. Which I am trying to do. The funny thing is he doesn't know I fight my natural urge to leave too! I just don't pack. Once I realized he wasn't going to stop me from packing. I vowed to never pack my shit again unless I meant to leave him for good. I don't have a problem leaving anyone, trust me. It was my strongest defense mechanism. I can deal with people in small doses. In relationships both my partner and I were always busy, so spending time meant something special. But when my partners wouldn't make spending time (free time we both shared), a priority, I flipped out! I felt abandon. So, I would break up with them after the third time! Hurt you before you hurt me. So, yeah, I know how to split in a flash. What I am currently learning/ trying to do is STAY! STAYING IS VERY DIFFICULT, when the person you love also want to destroy you! I mean one-minute shit is fine. The next, he says something and catches an attitude about something I said, did, or he "thinks" I said or did. Like when he puts shit somewhere and then looks at me as if I moved it. Makes slick ass comments and questions me like I would purposefully fuck with him like that! That is annoying. Again, he thinks poorly of me. But he's the one having hissy fits about being thought of bad!*

12. *Dude can't take a joke! I agreed that we have separate covers because I said he steals all the blankets at night. I remember that day. We were joking back and forth about freezing at night. I didn't know he would literally make sure we have two fucking blankets separating us from each other! Here I thought it was because my skin sticks to his and he doesn't like it. He said it makes him feel like something is crawling on him. No one is perfect, but Christ! So why do we beg perfection from each other!*

March 17, 2016

Life became too cruel. Love is just as violent as hate. There is no peace or solace on here, Earth. So, to Hell's gate I wait. For I know Christ will not forgive me taking my own life. Love you all enough to leave forever, Buttons.

My name is Buttons, I took Lorazepam .5mg about 30 pills. I should be dead by morning. If I am please call my daughter Mama: 860-------. She is to contact our family funeral director. I have a $50,000 policy through Woodmen at Connecticut nonprofit. Mama I texted you the passcode.

(Flashback) We were good friends. I helped Phi with his daughter. Phi used to come hangout at my house. Now, the whole time we were "JUST" friends, we would talk about his current relationship or emotional outburst on Facebook. SIDEBAR! People are watching your Facebook page! Potential employers, current employers, friends, family members, and associates. If you don't want the world to know your REAL feelings or emotional outburst DO NOT POST IT ON FACEBOOK!

Phi seemed to be a nice guy who was struggling with being a single-father when I met him. I missed all the red flags, because my heart refused to believe people can be so cruel or dysfunctional. I forgot about he emotionally came undone on Facebook. I forgot he had oral sex with KT. I can't tell you all that went on, because I was heavily sedated with the medication I was on. Question, do you ignore the worst in people? Why? Why not? Write them down in the back of the book. I hope this is helping you figure out some patterns and behaviors too.

*(Flashback) If you don't want to be bothered with the person you are with anymore TELL THEM. One day I got all three of them together, while Q was living with me, to tell me what happened. It was a healing experience that made everyone responsible for their actions. Turns out China never told Q it was broken off **before** she started seeing Phi. As a result, Q told everyone Phi had an incurable disease. Not that it stopped anyone from wanting to be with Phi, but it was vicious nonetheless. Once the fellas new that China tried to play them, they really began to get along. It was a miracle that Yaweh allowed me to be a vessel to see forgiveness and brotherly love. (Flashback over)*

What happened a month after that brotherly love experience would shock you! During this time Q and I had dated for about a month, from July to August. Q then informs me he wouldn't have a place to live after the first week of September, because his dad sold the house. This was risky on my part; however, I wasn't aware of my true self at the time.

I invited Q to come live with me. After all this brotherly and new-found friendship between Q and Phi. I thought Q was a decent dude and so I let him live with me. It lasted from September to November. Q and I broke up because he tried to attack me. Phi was there and helped me during this situation. A few weeks later Phi and I started dating. I do apologize for jumping around. My mind is a collection of experiences. I want to share so much but what to share when is difficult. Like I stated before, I make simple things a little complicated lol.

There are more journal dates during this chaotic time with Phi in Nevada. All this lead up to May 12, 2016 when he nearly beat me to death for crying about my daughter not wanting to have anything to do with me. He got mad because he couldn't comfort my broken heart over my daughter. Instead of letting me feel my emotions and making coffee. He turned it into a situation about him and then Phi hit me, grabbed me and slammed me on the floor. Phi slammed me so hard I broke our kitchen table with my back. He then proceeded to punch me in my throat, face, ribs, and head. My only thought was, "It was finally over."

Everything went black for moment. Then I heard a voice say, "NO!" I pushed my right foot into his chest. I stepped on his chest and grabbed my purse. My thought became, "I have purpose. I am going to live." If it were not for God! I would be dead.

This part of the conversation is hard. I understand. What we all need to know is this happens every day to women and men, by their lover, spouse or significant other. Many are too scared to leave. Others are too scared to talk. While still so many are dead. Make a commitment to yourself. NEVER let anyone treat you like their punching bag! Promise me! Promise me no matter what the situation or circumstance you will go. It is safer to leave than stay and die. You are worth living and hoping in. I trust you will move forward stronger than before, a little bruised, yet you will live!

When I ran away from Phi. I found myself at Droopy Drawers house. The house was packed with family. My Mom was there. I was safe but very emotional. I stayed for ten days with my family. I spent my 44th birthday with my sisters. It was nice. Droopy Drawers and I spent most of the time talking about spirituality and faith.

One day I was staring at my Mom. I secretly wished her dead. I blamed her for my mishap. I blamed her for all the abuse I ever received. While I was staring at her, she turned and looked at me with a smile. It was a look that stated, "I know what you are thinking." I laughed out-loud. It was a moment of understanding. I didn't want to hurt her. I just wanted the pain to stop. The pain that began for me at five years old. In time, through therapy and self-forgiveness the pain will end. At least I hope it will.

I left my sister's house and headed back to Connecticut. I was going to stay with Candy. Candy sent me the money to leave Phi in Nevada on May 12, 2016. I am heading home to reboot my life again. It is here I hope to get the supportive surroundings I need to recover.

❖

It's Friday, August 12, 2016 and I just finished visiting Roy. He is doing well. I told him about needing to end the connection to Todd my own way. It was simply by saying 'Thank You' in the spirit of gratitude. Now I feel lighter and what he did doesn't matter. What matters is the lessons I learned. These lessons will make me a better person with wisdom from the experiences.

Buttons and Droopy Draws October 2016

Writing a book isn't all that easy to do. Even if the topic is of self! It is an unusually difficult task to write down your past, present and hopes for the future. It is very emotional and causes ups and downs. Given that I have chronic depression and anxiety doesn't help. Perhaps this book will save me from a former self-image, while enhancing a greater more attuned self-image? Or maybe just maybe, I am supposed to be a famous author and you will be one of my greatest fans? Only the Universe knows at this point. I began writing to clear the clutter in my mind about what happened to me in California. How I became a homeless, 44-year-old woman, sleeping in a shelter? I wrote a brief essay about it. Days have turned into weeks and I have struggled to write. There are so many painful realizations of the choices I have made. None more than self-rejection. I have rejected who I am for so long just to belong.

Have you ever sacrificed your morals and ethics just to be part of someone or something? Have you ever tried to fit in to feel loved? I have. I have traded my True Self for my family, friends, and even religious beliefs. What I know to do for myself I didn't do it. When my gut or instincts told me to do otherwise, I didn't listen. There are warning signs I ignored. I don't have to be homeless. The decisions I made based on wanting to belong have put me in this situation. Had I listened to myself, I wouldn't be here. Or would I? I remember when I wanted out of the spotlight. I remember when I moaned and complained about being known and how it was too much pressure. Again, what I wanted was to just be myself. Now I am in an environment where no one knows me. No one expects anything of me. I am a "Nobody". I cannot say I like it or not. It just is. What will happen to me if I get back to a place where my name and face is recognized? If I do it on my own, with my True Self there should be no problem. I can be my silly, masculine, feminine, and intellectual self. This is the purpose of writing a book. To let people know me in my daily life and from my past. What makes a person go from being on top of their game to being part of the less desirable of society? Social pressure and expectations I say. How do I seem to those who know me or knew me? Do I look like a user? Do I look like a Leech? Or am I a pain in the butt? Whatever the character description, my image of myself, is one of a champion. I can be famous, infamous, or nothing at all. Who I am left with is up to me. No one can dictate my future but me.

I had to accept a great many things about myself on this journey. There are parts of my life I haven't fully disclosed because that is a tale for another book. What I am most proud of these days is my ability to discern people's motives. That includes my motives for dealing with individuals as well. Like why am I cleaving to my sister Droopy Drawers? Why am I cleaving to Mo?

Mo is my spiritual brother. I met him while visiting a church in Hartford, CT. We talk on the phone mostly every day. He knew something was wrong with me. He prayed and waited patiently for me to reach out, when I was in California. When I called, he said praise Jesus. Mo and I mostly converse about the Word of God and other religious beliefs. We talk a little about politics and relationships. Mostly, we talk about God.

That's why it was simple for me to answer those two questions. I love them both and I don't have to hide my true self. I talk with them about different aspects of me. I listen to them as they reveal different aspects of their true selves. It is refreshing! I spent so many months, days, hours, minutes, believing people appreciated my knowledge, love, and friendship. The truth is WE ALL EXPECT something in return for our time. Even if it's acceptance to be our true self.

I am writing my day-to-day thoughts and actions. If you or someone you know has days like mine. Please talk to a professional. Well, my chronic PTSD, severe depression and anxiety mind works different. There are days I still cannot believe I don't want to be around people. I shake, I stutter, I get super nervous. I can't believe I use to speak to thousands of people on a regular basis. Then there are those moments when everything seems okay. I love those moments.

Right now, I am just trying to figure out why do I shake so much around people. Why is this happening to me? My worst fear come realized. I lost my mind. Now I am fighting to get it back better than before.

My Day-to-Day Recordings

I wonder as I give you a glimpse of my daily life if you accept yourself? I am no longer afraid if you accept me or not. I am more afraid if you don't accept yourself. Why? Because you too can and will make decisions that can harm you or others if you don't. Others includes me! What is the foundation of your decision-making skills? Are you motivated by fear? Faith? Love? Hate? Are you motivated by emotional attachment or intellectual bondage? What is your purpose? People who settle for the day-to-day and find happiness are lucky. They have manifested the mediocrity of being on Earth. I once desired the same thing. As a little girl I wanted the handsome husband, white picket fence around my house, children and a sense of security. I wanted to have that loving, gentle, unwavering love of a man. To have financial security and take family vacations to Disney Land. I wanted to be a good wife, friend, and partner to my husband. The problem in my past is I would have it in abusive ways. Why? Because I was used to it. Todd once told me I didn't have what it takes to stay for the long haul. I know I can stay through good and bad. I just refuse to stay through abuse! Why is it that people think it is love if they beat on you; verbally, mentally, and emotionally abuse you? I will not and cannot stick through that! Does that make me less than an adequate partner? I don't think so. In that case, NO, I cannot stick it through with an abusive partner! I deserve better. I know that exist for me. It will manifest in time. The healthier I become the healthier the choices I make.

On August 21, 2016, I accepted that at 44 I am homeless and living in a shelter. I have lived in the shelter for three weeks. My new office space is the Danbury Library Technology area. I am grateful to have the space. What I am praying for and earnestly hoping is I have my own apartment by September 1, 2016. This of course would take a move of God in my favor. There are people who have jobs living in the shelter. Most have been there three months to almost a year with no housing. I'm hoping to get an apartment in a week! You will know how this all turns out. It's funny writing about your daily activities, while telling the story about parts of your life. I never thought I find myself unable to work due to fear and anxiety of human interactions. I can deal with small groups of ten people that I know. But if I don't know them, I can only tolerate five people max. Mixed crowds cause me to have major ticks/shakes. This is my life...living with PTSD and psychosomatic-seizures. Despite that, I will find balance and a way to enjoy life. To live and not survive.

I still haven't finished the book. So, to keep you updated on what is happening I will share with you some more moments. Today is Saturday, September 3, 2016. It is a Saturday filled with promise of hope, love and abundance. My attitude is more positive now that I am doing daily affirmations. I look for symbols of God's love and the presence of Angels around me. My outlook is brighter. Even though I didn't get my apartment, nor did I receive my Social Security Disability. Both are coming to me.

On Tuesday, August 30, 2016, my therapist and I requested to have my Social Security Disability case expedited. I also found out that my application for Mental Health Section 8 will be heard on Wednesday, September 7, 2016. As I see it the Universe/God is working in my favor. All things are done in a time that is set in my purpose. Now as I sit getting here ready to do group at the shelter, I realize I am safe and I have food.

What I am learning is to increase my vibrations to higher frequencies. Why? Because all my basic needs are met, just at a lower frequency. I have shelter, sleeping on a cot at the city shelter or living in my car. I have food, eating at the soup kitchen or using my food stamps and eating in my car. I have clothes, those I have managed to keep through this ordeal. If the basic needs of my human existence are being met at the lowest denominator, then I can believe my basic needs will be met at a higher frequency. Law of Attraction, Law of Nature, Law of Universe, and Law of Physics. The truth is the truth. I spoke basic words and manifested this basic life.

When I said I wanted to not have to worry about bills, food, or performing for society. I didn't mean have a nervous breakdown, become homeless, lose everything and try to killer yourself while your at it. I meant having enough money and resources, so I never have to live hand to mouth again. I can travel at will. I can do research on subjects I think are important. I can write books. Tell my story.

Now I am speaking abundance words and shortly I will have an abundant life. How this abundance will manifest is up to the Universe and my ability to speak Law of Attraction, Law of Nature, Law of Universe, and Law of Physics language in my daily communications. It is difficult, because of the way it is explained seems very obtuse and yet direct. You really don't know until you experience the epiphany moment when it all connects.

My advice is to read everything on these Laws. Try out some of the meditations that are provided on YouTube. Invest in your ability to grasp these concepts. When you do you can manifest the life you really want to live. Just remember each person's destiny or reality is different. Not everyone is going to win the lotto. Not everyone is going to be famous. Be honest with your true desires not your fantasies. Be a dreamer, by all means. Just make sure your dreams line up with the God's/Universe's plans.

3 At Mount Rushmore heading to California

September 4, 2016 is the day it began to make sense about my fear of heights. I was talking to Droopy Drawers, something I do daily, when we began discussing our childhood in Bristol, Connecticut. Specifically, we discussed the day I broke my Right foot! It was one of the many times we were put on punishment by our Mom. We were to stay in our rooms until she let us out. Droopy Drawers told me that I was very brave and wasn't afraid of heights. As she puts it, "Buttons, you weren't afraid of ANYTHING! Today, I have a fear of falling from high places. While talking about the great adventure Droopy Drawers thought I should write it in this book. Perhaps it will heal me from my fear of heights and falling from high places. This story is a combination of two memories, hers and mine.

Being Spider Woman

It was early evening and after being in the room for a week, Droopy Drawers, Peaches and I were restless. There were two white girls who lived with us and we all decided to play catch with the second-floor kids. We lived on the third floor of the building complex in Bristol, CT. I created many great adventure games and life for the most part was good. We had food to eat; clean clothes; and my Mom wasn't yelling at us all the time. I remember being happy and just being a kid for once. Life was good.

One of my bright ideas backfired on me. As a result, I ended up in the emergency room. Here is my attempt to be Spider Man/Woman in order to avoid a beating, lol.

I banged on the bedroom floor to get the kids below attention. I screamed from the window, "We going to play catch! Don't drop my ball!" The kids downstairs agreed, and the game began. I tossed the ball down and they caught it. They tossed the ball up and we took turns in the window catching it. After a few times, the kids downstairs arms got tired. So for the next three tosses, I caught the ball because I wasn't afraid to hang out the window. What I did was brace myself with my feet on the wall. Then I let my body hang out the window as low as I could go! I trusted the strength in my legs to lift me back up. It was kind of like doing push-ups with just your legs. Up and down the ball went. Until it went down and hit the ground. "Oh shit! I got to get my ball or Mommy know we were playing on punishment," I said. Droopy Drawers looked scared. The fear of getting a beating took hold. I said, "I will be Spider Girl! Just lower me on the rope and I will climb back up. I need everyone to help me slide down." I went into the closet and put on my snow suit. I took the jump rope and wrapped it around my waist. Then everyone tied the sheets from our beds, and the blankets. Then we took the last rope and tied it to the sheets and the bed. "Okay, I am ready! You guys ready?" Peaches, Droopy Drawers and the two girls held on tight as I ventured out the third-floor window. I was doing really well. I tried to walk the wall of the building like a mountain climber would. Then there was a slip and I slide down a foot. No longer moving. I was stuck for thirty seconds, dangling between the floors. I didn't know what was going on. I was just hanging around, lol.

This is what Droopy Drawers told me. My Mom came into the room. Petrified of being discovered, everyone let loose the sheets but Droopy Drawers. Her little body was the only thing keeping me suspended mid-air. Droopy Drawers struggled to hold my weight, while the bed kept creeping closer and closer to the window. "What are you guys up to? Where is Buttons? I'm getting my belt!" my Mother shouted. My Mom runs to get the belt and comes back into the room swinging! As the belt hits Droopy Drawers' legs, she screams and lets me go! Down I crashed to the ground. I landed on my feet but forgot to tuck and roll. I heard a loud crack! My mother's boyfriend, Tommy came running around the corner. He asked me to stand up. I told him I couldn't. Tommy scoops me up and carries me up to the third floor. I was put on my bed and my mom came in to give me my beating'.

Droopy Drawers talked to me about the guilt she felt for letting me go. I told her it wasn't her fault. No one should have let go! If anything, everyone should have held on until I was at the bottom or close to it! We laughed long and hard at this adventure that went awry. The real problem wasn't in the idea. No, the problem was I should have made one of them do it because I was the strongest person in the room! Lol. Looking it over it was a great childhood scheme that would have made for an excellent story, IF I made it down and back without being notice.

September 7, 2016 is a day for the records of my mother's abusive behaviors! As Droopy Drawers and I were talking today about our childhood. She shared something with me that was quite disturbing even dare I say FUCK UP! Luckily, I was going to my first Trauma Therapy with my new therapist. Boy, I tell you if I wasn't writing these things down I would show nuff be crazy! Lol. Technically, I am a little anxious, chronically depressed and have chronic PTSD, besides that I would be hospitalized if it were not for writing this book, lol!

Turns out my Mom, Wanda is a Pedophile, too! You see Droopy Drawers and I discussed how Tommy, the one who carried me up to the third floor, use to take pictures of us as little children. These pornographic photos included taking pictures of me with one of his sons. I was forced to have oral sex with one of Tommy's sons. What kind of woman allows these things to happen to her children, SMH?

Well I took that information and went to therapy. My question, "How does a mother do that to her children?" The answer, "She's a sick twisted woman!" The more profound and worse question is, "WHY THE HELL GRAMS KEPT GIVING US BACK TO HER!!!!" I'm just going to reflect on the conversation and the therapy session that left me feeling kind of lost in that time. I had to "ground" myself. Tell myself I was safe. Safe from who and what I don't know.

Today, **September 9, 2016**, was an AMAZING morning! My phone called Droopy Drawers, while I was talking to Mo! We had a three-way conversation. This is the first time they both were on the phone together. I sat back quiet and let them chat for about forty minutes. Today is also the day after Droopy Drawers and I were on a worldwide webinar to get our Soul's cleanse by Kari Samuels, from numerology.com. Yes, we both were on the same webinar and had two totally yet similar experiences. Droopy Drawers had different images flashing before her. I had three separate memories come to the front and had to let go of two of those memories, while replacing it with the third.

I'll give you the details of what happened to me. Kari Samuels began to walk us through her Four Steps to Activating Soul-Level Abundance through this meditation. First you have to surround yourself in light and call on Archangels, Spirit Guides and your own Guardian Angels. Second, you identify your blockers. Then you cleanse yourself from negative blockers at the Soul-Level. Finally, you replace the empty space with Love and Light and positive reconditioning.

My blockers involved my mother. The first one was when she was taking us "school shopping" with her boyfriend's nieces and nephews. They were acting up in the car, getting on her nerves and my sisters and I kept getting yelled at for it. When we finally got to the department store, my mom turns to us saying, "You three bitches aren't getting shit! I'm going to take this money and spend it on John's family!" Of course, my siblings and I began to cry. This moment reminded me of several experiences when shopping with her. Everywhere we went she always made us go to the cheap items and told us we didn't deserve shit. Amazing how comments and moments like these keep us from manifesting our true destiny. If one is constantly told he/she doesn't deserve goodness you learn to live within those limited parameters in your present and future.

Well last night I got rid of those negative blockers. I replaced those negative times with the meditation suggestions, while holding onto the memory of Rusty Jones taking us to the store to buy bikes. Really whenever we went anywhere with Rusty Jones he called us his Princesses and told us we deserve the world. Money seemed to flow easily to Rusty Jones and thus it flowed easily to us. I replaced a very evil experience around money and purchasing, with a blessed one. This has already changed my perspective in life. Right now, I am ready to end this story and start another book. I will not end it while I'm still waiting for the check from Social Security disability and living in the shelter. I also want to write that I won MegaMillions' jackpot on this day. How's that for life changing! We all need a happy ending to inspire us to move forward and have hope. It is my desire that this topsy-turvy, manic ride of a book, not only gives insight into my life, but provides you hope that you too can overcome.

I love lotus flowers because this particular plant species describes for me, the reasons for my former challenges in life. It is not by happen stands that I endured some of these horrific events. It was the cards I was dealt in order to help someone else heal. I'm not a saint. I am an optimistic healer. I have my own gifts and talents. Some have been abused by others. While most laid dormant until now.

Like the lotus flower, which grows in the swamp. Its roots are deep in that murky water. What we see as a delicate and exotic flower. Began in the mud. How my life began. Is not how it will end. I am blooming I am a Lotus Flower.

I look forward to us continuing our conversation over the next several years. My life, Your life, Our lives are journeys. What we hope for without blockers can and will come to pass. What we dream and love with our healed hearts will manifest in our daily lives. I know good and great things are ahead. Believing in the impossible is not foolish. If you can believe in the worse, why not believe in the best. It is better for you. Until the next time we speak. God's love shines upon you, in you and through you. Living in Love and Light, Buttons.

The Journals

What is thought?

By LaResse Harvey 2017

What is thought to you?

Thought is a process of information that conforms an idea that can become real eventually.

Where does it come from?

Thoughts comes from within our subconscious and conscious mind. I believe thought is our inner self communicating to the Universal what we most desire.

I desire Love, Light, Money, Wealth, Healing, Freedom to be ME.

God thought about it; said it; made it happen.

Thought becomes our reality.

Thought is action.

Thought is my manifestation of my present and future.

What is thought?

One Year after California

July 30th, 2016

One year since I was last employed due to my psychosomatic-seizures. I am still waiting for Social Security Disability to approve me. I was at the library today for about 50 minutes. Candy dropped me off and told me she would be back at 1pm, when the library closes. There is a fair on the Green, in between the library and the post office. Candy told me to walk to the post office, the van would be parked there. (Now, I was hoping she would realize there are a great deal of people.) Meaning, my psychosomatic-seizures happen mostly when I am around large crowds and strangers. It's a little tricky to explain, but I will try.

I left the library at 1pm and waited at the top until 1:05pm. Then I walked down to the sidewalk from the library path. I looked for the van prior to crossing the street. I walked across the street onto the Green and three steps in, my head starts twitching fast. I am attempting to pass people as quickly as possible BEFORE my whole body goes. I make it to the post office in fifteen more steps. I look in the parking lot. No Candy, no van. I am twitching and now I have to walk through the Green again. "This is INSANITY Buttons. You cannot have anyone drive you anywhere anymore. You need to escape and feel safe at a moment's notice. That is not anyone's responsibility but yours." This is the conversation I had with myself as I walk down the sidewalks to cross the street. It's the way home and that is where I am headed.

I told Candy I didn't have my cell phone. I don't think she remembered. I wait on the corner for another five minutes. Looked up the street and the seven cars coming up the one way. Well, I don't see her and it's 1:15pm. I started walking home. I wasn't upset with Candy. I just wished I had my phone, so she wouldn't worry I hope she knows to just go home. At least that is what I was taught growing up. If you lose someone in the crowed, starting driving or heading towards home. The fastest route there. I guess, she panicked and couldn't think. I will never know the real level of anxiety it caused. I did apologize. I am not staying anywhere that makes me shake. If you say you are going to be there at a certain time than be there. Again, not her fault. I am the ONLY person that knows and cares about my psychosomatic-seizures every minute of the day. No one else. Having an invisible disability, until it becomes visible is a drag.

I hope through reading my journal you begin to understand how fragile my mind has become. There are days I feel like I know what direction I am going. Other days, I feel lost, confused and don't want to live. I keep asking the same question, "Why has so many painful traumatic things happened to me? Are you there God?" I am sure you have asked God/Universe why things happened to you.

August 5, 2016

What a difference 24 hour can be! I am now living in a shelter in Danbury. Candy and I had a minor argument that turned major for our friendship. Let's just say.... having a substance abuse issue is deadly for the user and the bystander! I'm just sick to death of people who say they LOVE ME and ONLY abuse me! Hurting people HURT people is true! Hurting people hurt themselves more than others. I just couldn't continue to be dismissed like I was a five-year-old child. Besides, why did she keep hanging up on me? I don't get people who do not want to resolve conflicts. Don't you understand that if the conflict isn't discussed it turns into resentment? Well Candy hung up the phone on me twice. I turned my car around and headed back to the house. I know, you are wondering what happened, lol. I will explain in a few moments. When I got to the house Candy "pretended" not to be there. She was hiding in the house somewhere. I went upstairs to wait for her. My intuition told me to start packing because she was going to kick me out. Lucky for me I LISTENED!

I couldn't fit everything into the bags I had upstairs. I left to go to the store and purchase garbage bags. When I returned to the house, Candy was making a mad dash to her van. I said, "Candy, I am leaving." Her response was priceless, "Get your shit out my house. By the time I get back all your fucking shit better be out!" Then Candy started to whimper, "All I needed was a friend." "No, what you need is help," I said as I walked into the house. I continued to pack and then called my friend Treena to see if I stay at her house for the night.

I mean really, why wake someone up over a comment from a stranger, unless the statement is true? You can call me a Crack Head all day. I won't be upset. I will just keep laughing at you. Well, it will get annoying and I might snap, but not the first 50 times. So, that was the end of my friendship with Candy.

I spent two months living with her. I thought she understood what I was going through. I dealt with strangers coming to stay at her house she just met. I dealt with her crazy siblings and her ups and downs. I even dealt with her emotional drunk confessions at night. Just think, I was going to acknowledge her for allowing me space to write my completed book. Now her acknowledgment belongs amongst all those others who have caused me unnecessary pain. I mean you don't need an excuse to kick someone out your house. Just tell them to leave. The problem is your motives for wanting them gone. You see, I believe Candy started doing drugs. Which would explain her irritating, impatience new attitude. Either way, it's another trauma added to the list of this past years HELL.

August 21, 2016

Today I accepted that at 44, I am homeless and living in a shelter. I'm not to be moved until God moves me. I have to learn to be content in all things. I have shelter (a place to sleep and my car), food (soup kitchen and food stamps), and the clothes I have managed to keep with me through all my transitioning. I must be still and trust that God will provide me with what I need. I've had money and used it to make others happy. I believed that would make me happy. I've had shelter and didn't appreciate it. I cannot live in the past. I must stay in the present. I can't worry about the future. Tomorrow may never come. All I have is today. Today I can choose to be happy. Today I can find hope. Today I can trust God to place me in the perfect environment within my means. Today I can receive God's love in abundance. Just for today, I will trust and receive love from within and above.

August 22, 2016

I dislike the lethargic side effects of my new medication. I sat and spoke with a few people from the shelter. We laughed together about a few things. All of us decided life was good because we are one day closer to leaving the shelter. I can laugh again. I can joke again. It's nice to be okay and love me today. I want my own place. I need my own place. God will provide it when He decides. I am not waiting on anyone or anything, except God. Ellegua, Yamaye, and Ochun are helping me. Today I feel the earth moving towards me and lifting me out of darkness and poverty. My Facebook message was answered. I had physical, emotional and mental reaction. I still love him regardless of what I believe he has done to me. I can love unconditionally. That's what Todd taught me over the eight years I worked with him. I have closure. He left the choice to reconnect up to me. I know I will get good news in the mail soon regarding my social security disability. Let it begin with a check and approval letter, Amen.

August 23, 2016

Today is a cold morning. I'm about to go to group. I feel sluggish. I think I will just take my Buspar and call it a day. Yesterday was a message day. The message… "Love Conquerors All!" God is love and His love for me is sufficient in all things no matter what it looks like. Today I pray with faith I have my social security disability approval. I have housing that is private, comfortable, clean, roach and rat free with gas and electric included. I pray for an apartment that has a front and back door. A place that is surrounded by the view of nature, trees and animals. A place where I can rest my mind and my body. A place I can write my books. A place big enough for when my grandchildren come over we have space. Small enough to be intimate. My heart's desire is a one bedroom. However, I will accept a Studio if God wants me there. I just need to get out of this shelter. Not because it's bad. I want to leave so I can sleep. Perhaps I will have better luck finding help at New Horizons.

August 26, 2016

Today I realized that I almost died twice, because of my love for Mama. The first time was in 1993 when Tabitha said she was coming back to kill my children, (her and Budda). The second time was on May 12, 2016, the day after she dismissed me and said I was verbally abusive and she wasn't going to take it anymore, like she did when I was married. The worst part is I'm in therapy group with folks that have no fucking idea about real life struggle. They believe I'm violent and aggressive! My fucking ass! The truth is if I can't find a place to express myself then I will explode. I can blame my daughter all day. I can even cry about our broken relationship. The problem with that is how accepting I am with my daughter's decision to disown me. There is no reason no matter what fucking words I choose for her to treat me this way. So now, I am moving forward without her or Budda in my heart. From this point on, they will need to come to me and apologize for their behaviors towards blaming me for shit I had no control over.

September 8, 2016

During meditation I thought about how shopping with my Mom was always a hit or miss. On this particular day, she told my sisters and I we were not worthy of new clothes. We were school shopping with one of her boyfriends and his nieces and nephews. Mom took our school clothes money and spent it on them. Every time we went to the store with Mom, she always belittled us and made us feel like we only deserve the minimum. She always called us ungrateful or bad bitches. Rusty Jones on the other hand, would treat us like princesses. He would tell us we are valuable and deserve the best. He always gave us an abundance of money. There were few store moments with Rusty Jones. He really wasn't around that much after the divorce. Sometimes, he would pick us up to occupy is girlfriend's children, lol. I never felt broke or unworthy around him. Strange….

September 9, 2016

Around 9:30pm I had a psychosomatic seizure. I felt it coming on. I felt dizzy, nauseous, and light headed. I took a shower and fifteen minutes later it happened. I started twitching and jerking around. It was minor, because it lasted only five minutes. I haven't had a serious seizure since August 3rd, 2016 the day before Candy kicked me out her house. Nothing specific happened today. It was my normal routine.

September 12, 201

Did Mind Movie meditation with Natalie Ledwell. Learning to eliminate self-limiting beliefs. What are my self-limiting beliefs? "Fear of Failure or Fear of Success"? I should have spent time thinking about this. Right now, I am afraid of everything and everyone. I keep dreaming about people attacking me. When I walk into a store I keep my head down out of fear someone will make eye contact and attack me. I wish I could go back to thinking everyone was good, smh.

I used to be an optimistic person until this mental illness. I was outgoing. I mean I would hug people when I first met them. Everyone to me was like family. Now I am scared to look at people let alone shake a hand.

September 17, 2016

Today I woke up and thought about my former boss and how she fired me. I was so angry and hurt I began seizing in my bed. I despise her for what she did to me. I was very angry. I want her to die and all that she built, be destroyed. I want her to be exposed for the gambling, double-talking hustler she really is!

Then I began to realize those thoughts will not hurt her and her program will do harm if it doesn't exist. So, I took a deep breath and exhaled. Letting it all go. She is no different than most inconsiderate people in this world. It isn't her fault she doesn't care or realize the severity of her actions. Vengeance is the Lord's job not mine. Today I am letting her go and the damages she caused my mind, body, and spirit. No longer will I burden my soul with the anguish that she caused. There is no comprehension. There is just knowledge that some people on Earth come more negative than positive. I let it go!

4 My last Drug Policy Alliance Conference

September 18, 2016

I am at the park in my favorite spot looking at the mountain, while sitting in my car. I did my meditation to heal myself from money blockers. Droopy Drawers and I have made a decision. When I get my social security disability money, I will fix my car and then head to her house. At least I know my sister won't kick me out. While we talked I discovered a few things. 1. Regardless as to what happens I'm leaving Connecticut on October 6, 2016. There is no need for me to stay in Connecticut. Mama has her life and the grandchildren knows I love them and they love me. I need to take care of myself. Bouncing around and staying at a shelter is not helping me and my mental state. It is time to move forward. I don't know what God/Universe has planned for me. What I hope for and desire is a life filled with financial security, love, hope, and peace. I want to be a Spiritual Healer. I want to be a famous author/writer. I want to publish my first book. All of this is my desire. I am taking action now. I have finished a rough draft of my book. I have people reading it from different socio-economic backgrounds. Once I put their suggestions into the book I will finish my first masterpiece. I have hope. I don't have to be a misfit or be in a place I am not safe and secure. I have dreams again. I don't want to do anything but relax. And write, meditate or pray if I choose. I want my home to be my private spiritual haven. Home…it's a very important word…Droopy Drawers is right. I don't need an apartment and the responsibility of managing too much right now. I am grateful she is my sister and best friend. Whether I get social security disability or not. I won't be in a shelter anymore or ever again. I have hope today. That's what I need to hang onto…HOPE. Faith is the substance of things hope for. The evidence of things unseen. What is substance? What is hope? What is evidence? Let's find out!

Substance – A material or a particular kind; the quality of being meaningful, useful, or important. **Ultimate reality that underlies all outward manifestations and change.

Hope – To want something to happen or be true and think that it could happen or be true: to cherish a desire with anticipation; to desire with expectation of obtainment

**to expect with confidence: Trust

Evidence – something which shows that something else exists or is true. A visible sign of something. An outward sign. Something that furnishes proof.

Faith – is the substance (ultimate reality that underlies all outward manifestations and change), of things Hope (to expect with confidence, TRUST) for. The evidence (a visible sign of something; an outward sign) of things unseen.

I've been battling mental health issues and pretending to be like everyone else, most of my life. I have been a chameleon to fit in. That's why things shift and change in my life. Until now I was what people expected me to be. Give me the rules and regulations and I will perform until I can't. Do I have faith? Did I have faith? What is the difference between now and then? I have always behaved and therefore believed in that model of behavior. Those former versions of myself were not totally real. Therefore, my faith was circumstantial. Today I do believe I have faith. I need more evidence while I wait, but I have faith. How do I decide what evidence is of good value vs. bad or is it useless information? Am I listening to God? Am I just doing what is comfortable to me? There were days I felt suicidal and stayed on the phone with my sister. I believe that if you kill yourself, you will go to HELL. I struggle with wanting to live and wanting to die because the pain is so bad! I wish I could bounce back and move forward. This time I can't!

September 19, 2016

Tonight, I was in the shelter taking a shower. When I got out, I was standing in front of the closed door naked. One of the ladies came in the opposite door. That was cool because you couldn't see me. After she used the bathroom, she tried to open the door towards the dorm, where the men can look and see me naked! I told her to go out the other door. She went out the other door. I hurried up and got dressed. Then walked to my bunked and prayed. Not sure if I was being assertive or aggressive. What's the difference? Is it the tone?

Anyway, ever since this particular chic came back into the shelter, I've been twitching and seizing. People make me nervous. Unstable people make me very nervous. I can take my medication and still twitch like crazy. I don't even like talking to people except to be cordial. Not trying to make friends here or looking for a life partner. Just want to be by myself. Then I know I am safe and have peace.

79

September 20, 2016

One of the guys asked me to help them fill out a simple form. I had a difficult time concentrating. I started to shake and sweat. I had to stop five times on the first page. It was basic information. I'm not getting better. I am getting worse. I can't think. Seems like any type of confrontation or questioning triggers me. I can't wait until I leave Connecticut. I will visit my grandchildren and that's it. I am afraid all the time. Will this ever end?

September 21, 2016

Good morning Yahweh! I woke up feeling super. I had a great night sleep. All I smelled was frankincense and myrrh! I got up once only to turn over in my cot. I had a wonderful dream about my book. The thought of being interviewed filled my heart with joy. I wasn't in front of a large crowd. I was just sitting, and I can see people smiling at me. Today is going to be a good day.

September 24, 2016

It's time to deal with Rusty Jones and Mom. Not to blame them. I must explore what did they teach me? What do I need to set myself free of? What do I need to unlearn? At a young age I was the negotiator in their relationship. I became the protector to my mother, while she was pregnant with Droopy Drawers. This role continued even in the arena of the bedroom. I was called by my mother (protecting her wifely duties). I was put in my place (powerless, couldn't move or cry), by my dad when he fingered my innocent vagina. All the while my mom whispered lies to my young impressionable mind, "You are helping your father and me. You are saving our marriage." I was trained to believe I did have power to heal relationships. I did not know it wasn't my place. What my mother saw in me was a protector at two years old. I stood up to my abusive father for my unborn sibling, NOT for my mom.

If you take away my abuse what do I look-like to me? Who am I? What can I accomplish? Healing your soul is an easy choice. The journey is a difficult process. Does it matter I remembered my first traumatic experience? How do I heal and recover? How do I stabilize myself again enough to go on a job interview? To hold a job?

What does love feel like? Smell like? Taste like? What does love sound like? What does it really look like?

October 4, 2016

God has a plan for me. I just need to trust Him and it. An old colleague contacted me. He gave me credit for being on top of the Mass Incarceration connections to modern day slavery through the 13th Amendment. It made me smile. My visions and instincts are correct. I need to trust them more. The truth is God's plan is the only plan. Every time I plan my life it ends up in a big mess.

My mind is racing again. It is focused on the new political climate and the activities reformers can get involved in. I'm not current on what's being done. I just can see what can happen. Once again, I start twitching. I need to find my center. I'm not well enough to move on any issue. I need to focus on myself. I need to heal. In time what I understand and know will be useful. Right now, I cannot focus long enough without having a seizure.

October 6, 2016

I was asked to work at the shelter. I started to tick because I would have to deal with PEOPLE. The idea of people asking me question or getting things for them scares me. What if they grab me and I swing or worse have a seizure. Droopy Drawers reminded me that I will be leaving soon to be with her. I don't get why everyone is trying to get me to work! Just let me be mentally disabled until God says otherwise! Trust, I don't like it either. I've had my own money and paid my own way since I was fourteen. If I cannot focus without twitching, help or stand up for my own rights, trust my emotions, then I don't need to be in the workforce.

In therapy I realized I haven't dealt with what happened between Tamatha and I before I ever stabbed her when they jumped me. She's another person who betrayed my friendship and trust. I also realized that I have threaten many people throughout my life to protect myself. It was as if I could back them down with a threat. I wouldn't need to use my fist. I had developed a stare and a stand to ward off anyone who might hurt me. I'm not sure how long I've been threatening people to protect myself. I do know when I've stopped threatening people was last year. It was also the first time I was so mad and didn't hit the person that pissed me off. You don't know how drastic of a change that is until you reflect back.

Tammy was someone I was trying to help out of a situation. She pretended to need or want my help. Really she was out to destroy me. I don't know if she was ever sincere. What I do know was her vehement promise to kill me and my children was more powerful than her cry for help. If that was actually a cry for help? As far as I'm concern it was a ploy to get me to put my defenses down. Which I did. I never thought a person would be so hateful and cruel. I didn't think that a person could be hateful enough to pretend they were being abused, then turn around and want to kill the person helping them. Sad how it all turned out. I didn't like her boyfriend. I didn't want to have anything to do with him or his guns. She died over nothing. She died because she wanted to be a bad ass with her best friend. Another part of my innocence died that day too. I stopped really trusting people. I stopped loving strangers. I became more defensive and shielded.

At trial, the young Canadian Jamaican guy I was helping, testified for the prosecution in order to get his Green Card. Wow! I took Kirk into my home when he had none. I feed him and helped him find a job. My payback was Kirk setting me up. Why do I keep making the enemy of my well-being, my friend? Why can't I see people for who they really are before it causes me harm? I was twenty years old going on twenty-one. I was headed to Ohio to be with my siblings. No one was going to stop me. Kirk and Tabatha did! Kirk with his selfishness and Tammy with hers. I remember Tamatha standing over me, while her ugly ass boyfriend tried to beat me up on my own couch. I remember asking her for help to get him off me. She just stood there saying, "If she is lying why are you hitting her?" I don't understand why human beings are so hateful. Now I'm twitching again. This is a reality that even in my memory is too painful.

October 8, 2016

I was scared in California. I also didn't want to fail at another relationship. I went through three guys in one year. The last one was Phi. I stayed with him out of fear. I was living in a fantasy thinking I was smarter than he was. I could help him control his emotional outbursts and heal his insecurities. I could not! Another example of someone asking me for help, but really resenting me. When I had the opportunity to leave I didn't. I felt like I owed him something for helping me. My ego wouldn't let me go home without a fight. Not until my life was threaten. This is a constant struggle. From now on when my gut tells me someone is a negative overbearing emotional insecure person I am going to run far away from them.

October 9, 2016

I'm anxious about leaving before I get approved from social security disability. I want Droopy Draws to save her money. I hope I get approved before Thursday, when I leave. Janet turned out to be a great friend. She has helped me ever since I came back to Connecticut. I let her know I was leaving and she offered me a place to sleep the night before I left and some money. You never know who will be there for you during your darkest time. I appreciate her for her heart and honesty.

Meditation gives me the feeling of everything will work out. I have more than enough to be secure. I'm happy because today, I love myself. I desire to see me do something amazing to be worthy of love. Life is good, and I need to accept it.

October 10, 2016

Today is very cold and I don't have heat in this car. Thank goodness I have my brown wrap and purple blanket. It's crazy that there isn't any place for homeless people to go to keep warm, besides the library. I see Roy today to say bye. Thursday, I leave for Ohio and a different life. Droop Drawers says I need to rest for at least a year and heal. She believes I have wounds that have bled out over time. That's what she calls all the trauma I have suffered and pushed forward without addressing them, wounds. I have hope for a better life. At least I won't be in this shelter and freezing in my car for seven hours.

October 11, 2016

Last night's dream was about me having robotic children that were trying to kill me. I woke up twitching and couldn't shake the images. In my dream I was happily married. My life was good. I didn't want for anything and my husband was very loving. Then we wanted children. It was futuristic, so we ordered a boy and he tried to kill us by feeding us poison. Then we ordered a girl. She tried to kill us by making us choose who died first in a maze of glass. The third time we ordered a girl and she was standing over my husband with a knife. I don't know what all these attacking dreams mean. I just keep feeling like people are out to kill me or destroy me. I hope these nightmares will end soon. My heart is beating out my chest. These dreams seem so real. In just a few days I will be off to Ohio.

October 13, 2016

I woke up at Janet's house. It was nice to sleep in a bed and not a cot. I took a shower and said good-bye to her and her husband. I saw my psychiatrist, who gave me a new prescription. She filled out the form stating that because of my disability I am unable to work. Tonight, I will be in Ohio with Droopy Drawers. Life will begin anew.

I made it to Ohio. I literately felt a heaviness leave my shoulders. I am warm, and I have a bed to sleep in. I have my own room. On Monday, I will call social security disability. I made it and I am finally safe. Now I can focus on healing my wounds.

Moving Forward

How did I do in telling my story? Are you still engaged? Are you confused about any part of this conversation? As I stated before this is a unique conversation where I convey to you what my life experiences are as an abused child who grew up to be a woman with PTSD.

Moving forward Buttons is going to a safe environment around people who love her. I spoke to a lawyer who is going to fight for me. I was denied social security disability on October 2016. Now I am going to appeal the decision. I spent months waiting for an answer and feeling down about not having money to buy basic stuff like soap, deodorant and personal items. It was depressing. I fought suicidal thoughts because I believe myself worthless. Why? Because I cannot take care of myself financially. But there is HOPE.

I am moving to Ohio with Droopy Drawers. My sister is so excited to have me stay with her. Each day she tells me to just focus on healing. Each day she tells me she loves me. I didn't realize how much I need to hear those things until now. Can I really take the time to heal? Can I just be in one place and go to therapy? Can I just be? All I am asking is to heal. All Droopy Drawers wants is for me to heal. However long that takes, I am finally safe and able to totally focus on my healing. While I wait for Social Security Disability to decide. It is going to take about two years. I hope by the time we meet I would have won my case. Here is to projecting positive thoughts into the atmosphere. Another HOPE SHOT!

Taking a Break for Love

by LaResse Harvey

I'm taking a break.
I'm breaking out for Love.
I don't have to pressure myself and have it all figured out.
I don't have to be lazy crazy, dazy, or cunning.
I don't need to put it altogether,
When the promises are never forever.

I deserve a break.
I'm breaking out for Love.
I'm gonna let go of the rules and choose to be me.
Free from chains and souls that bind me.

I'm taking a break.
I'm breaking out for Love.
It's not about who's there or not;
Who loved or not
Who should've, could've, or would've or not.

I'm taking this break.
To give myself permission.
Permission to love the only human being that matters from above.

I'm giving myself a Break.
I'm breaking out for love.
I'm not confused nor am I someone's fool.

I deserve a break.
To take time to love.
Love that was given to me from above.

I am my break.
I'm breaking out to Love.
No second guessing;
No time for lessons.
I'm breaking out to love me.

Being A Strong Black Woman

What does it mean to be a Strong Black Woman? For me it meant chronic PTSD. I was doing research to understand what it meant to be a Strong Black Woman. It's funny how now they call it a "syndrome". Being a Strong Black Woman is a mental illness of selflessness and lack of self-care.

According to Florida A&M University College of Law: Black Women's Post-Slavery Silence Syndrome: A Twenty-First Century Remnant of Slavery, Jim Crow, and Systemic Racism--Who Will Tell Her Stories? Black women suffer from being silenced. This silence was introduced during slavery and exasperated into modern day stressors. The journal suggests cultural secrecy allows the woman to protect those who have abused them. An article written in BlackDoctor.com, describes a mother of two, with absent fathers, who doesn't take a day off nor asks for help. While she seems to have it all together underneath she was suffering. While taking care of others she failed to care of herself. Relationships began to deteriorate and there was no room for a love life. Her needs were silenced. They were silenced by herself, which allowed others to ignore her needs and view their own as more important. These conditions were followed by her "burning out" and breaking down. Just like I did.

The idea of taking care of ourselves as Black women is considered selfish and unbecoming. There were and are others who need us to be strong and move forward under any condition. I remember a time I was raped by a boyfriend, when my daughter was two years old. I am not sure if she seen any of the incident or not. What I remember is sitting in the corner thinking I was five and my father just "hurt" me. I was sucking my two middle fingers and crying. That's when MaMa walked up to me and simply said, "Ma milk!" while she waived her bottle in my face. I got up, wiped my tears, walked out the room and told my ex-boyfriend to leave and never come back. I never had him arrested nor did I get any therapy for the rape. I just functioned "as if" it never happened. I know I am not alone.

What happens when you cannot take it anymore? You break! There can be small breaks in health. Other breaks can be devastating. In my case, I couldn't handle being treated with disrespect, verbal and emotional abuse by employers and other colleagues, friends, and family members. This includes physical, sexual and mental abuse from lovers. My mind said, "NO MORE!" My heart began to weep and couldn't stop.

The childhood abuse I suffered only prepared or numbed me to handle degrees of abuse as comforting familiar emotions. Not realizing these are not normal. Over time the stressors became too great and I had a psychological break that included physical seizures. This gave me a diagnosis of Manic Depression, Severe Anxiety and Chronic Post Traumatic Stress Disorder with psychosomatic seizures.

Did you know 8% of Americans suffer from PTSD, according to PTSD United . That's the population of Texas! It is more common in woman than men to develop PTSD. The most common remark is, "So what. My life was hard too!" Life being hard isn't what causes Post Traumatic Stress Disorder. Society is sympathetic towards veteran PTSD and scoff at civilians diagnosed with the same condition. Society not showing compassion for the millions of Americans suffering from PTSD only traumatizes us further.

I hope my conversation with you has enlightened you to what it's like to have Post Traumatic Stress Disorder. I hope I have shown you that forgiveness isn't forgetting. It's making sure that you don't carry the pain of yesterday into your tomorrow. Mostly, I hope you understand the frailness of a mind that is suffering from a mental illness. Until the next Buttons' Journey...Be well and be gentle with yourself.

ABOUT THE AUTHOR

Button's Journey: My first two years living with PTSD, describes in detail the effects of long-term abuse and trauma. What happened to her as a child, prisoner, adult, and most importantly how she began to live again. Like the Lotus Flower, LaResse took her swampy, filthy experiences and used them to bloom. This is not her first time recreating a new positive image to inspire many and empower most. Button's Journey *(first in a series)*, tells a poetic story of hope and manifesting the life you deserve.

Formally incarcerated single mother, LaResse Harvey was the Director of Strategic Relations at A Better Way Foundation, a Connecticut nonprofit organization that works to establish reentry policies, substance abuse treatment, and overall public health model towards ending the war on drugs. As the Executive Director of Civic Trust Public Lobbying Company in Connecticut, she worked to support community legislative priorities by providing lobbying services free for members. Also, Ms. Harvey was the Criminal Justice Committee chair of New Britain NAACP chapter; Community Liaison on Connecticut Legislator's Eyewitness Committee; One of the national leaders on "Ban the Box", formally incarcerated people's campaign to remove incarceration question on job applications, known as the Fair Chance campaign.

Ms. Harvey advocated for the Children's Act of 1988 as a teen mom. In 2008, LaResse Harvey helped to put an end to Connecticut's '3-Strikes law' and published an article with the International Journal of Music promoting the importance of "The Arts" as a form of rehabilitation. Her vast sense of knowledge in policies to strengthen Connecticut's communities have helped greatly in reducing imprisonment and increasing reentry efforts. In 2011, Ms. Harvey successfully advocated and lobbied for Marijuana Decriminalization, 911 Good Samaritan, Sentence Modification, reestablishment of Good Time, National Recommendations to Eliminate Prison Rape, Credit Report discrimination, creation of the Department of Correction Advisory Committee and provide protection for expelled students to participate in adult education programs without being required to officially withdraw from school. As a lobbyist, Ms. Harvey has passed over fifty pieces of legislation and created the Speak Up! Speak Out! Advocacy toolkit that was translated into fifty-two languages. Legislation that helped closed three Connecticut prisons.

Ms. LaResse Harvey knows first-hand the importance of

community organization, advocacy, civic engagement and lobbying as tools to create change. Ms. Harvey has over ten years' experience working on issues of a women's right to choose, housing, reentry, drug treatment, and custodial parental rights. Ms. Harvey has four college degrees: three Associates Degrees from Tunxis Community College and a bachelor's in social work from University of Saint Joseph's College, West Hartford, CT.

In July of 2010, Harvey was awarded the Patriot Award from the Bill of Rights Defense Committee for her dedication in ensuring constitutional and human rights for all Connecticut residents. Ms. Harvey serves as a living example as to what an individual can offer, Hope, Change, and Second Chances.

Journal Your Thoughts

_____

_____

_____

_____

_____

_____

_____

_____

_____

_____

_____

_____

_____

_____

_____

_____

_____

_____

_____

_____

_____

_____

_____

_____

_____

_____

_____

_____

_____

_____

_____

_____

_____

_____

_____

_____

_____

_____

_____

_____

_____

_____

_____

_____

_____

_____

_____

_____

_____

_____

_____

_____

_____

_____

_____

_____

_____

_____

_____

_____

_____

_____

_____

_____

_____

_____

_____

_____

_____

_____

_____

_____

_____

_____

_____

_____

_____

_____

_____

_____

_____

_____

_____

_____

_____

_____

_____

_____

_____

_____

_____

_____

_____

_____

_____

_____

_____

_____

_____

_____

_____

_____

_____

_____

Made in the USA
Middletown, DE
01 July 2021